TRAVELS

AND

TRAVELLERS.

A Series of Sketches.

BY

MRS. TROLLOPE,

AUTHOR OF

" THE BARNABYS IN AMERICA," " THE ROBERTSES,"
" THE ATTRACTIVE MAN," ETC.

IN TWO VOLUMES.

VOL. I.

LONDON:
HENRY COLBURN, PUBLISHER,
GREAT MARLBOROUGH STREET.
1846.

GRÄFFENBERG.

GRÄFFENBERG.

WHEN contemplated a little *en masse*, that is, from a point sufficiently distant in time to give us a tolerably wide extent to look over, there is something almost comic in the variety of specifics which have been hit upon by poor blundering, but always onward-struggling man, for the remedy of the ills that he is heir to.

But though this may be the effect produced upon the idle looker-on, by the variety, not to say contrariety, of the means employed to achieve this great object, the attempt, whenever seriously and honestly made, is far too laudable, and too important also, to be treated lightly. A perfect catalogue of all the experiments tried to

"Make men well, when they are sick,"

could scarcely be perused with gravity; yet, with the above proviso, that they were made seriously and honestly, there would probably not be found one wholly unworthy of attention; and perhaps it may be doubted whether there has been more folly shown in the ignorant rejection, or in the ignorant adoption of some among them. The name of the remote, and, till recently, most obscure little hamlet of Gräffenberg, will now at once tell the reader, let him come from what quarter of the world he may, that the following pages are on the subject of the *water cure*, or, at any rate, on the place where it was first tried, and where its inventor has surrounded himself with an immense establishment, in the midst of which he resides, honoured as a sovereign, beloved as a benefactor, and, by many, almost worshipped as a saint.

The long-established habit of wandering during the summer months, made the idea of passing from Florence to Silesia a much less terrific thing to me than it would be to most people; and one of my family having been complaining of dyspepsia, and another friend, for whose health I was greatly interested, appearing to think that both the journey and the discipline might be beneficial to her, we set off, a party of four, from the fair City of Flowers, to travel about nine hundred miles to the north-east of it, for the sake of sounding the well, at the bottom of which Sir Edward Bulwer Lytton says that health is to be found.

Much short of nine hundred miles we could not have made the distance; but we, in our usual desultory style, contrived to make it considerably more. We certainly came now and then upon some detestably bad inns, where sundry divine creations of a less tranquil nature than sleep, visited our pillows; but excepting this occasional annoyance, the journey had more to please than weary. It is no great misfortune to be obliged to visit Bologna, Padua, and Venice, especially since a tolerably easy railroad has connected the two last. At Venice, however, I did find a real misfortune, in the shape of an artist who was employed by Louis-Philippe to copy the Assumption, and whose canvas *almost* concealed the glowing morsel of immortality of which it hoped to carry away the *reflet*. It is quite right in Louis-Philippe to endeavour to obtain a copy of the Assumption, but those who visit the gallery of the Belli Arti at Venice while it is about, are out of luck. I ought to have found comfort from remembering that I had seen it before; but such is the perversity of human nature, that I thought myself in a more pitiable condition than those of my party who knew not what they had lost.

The first unnecessary lengthening of our road which our errant fancies decided upon, was the coming by Innspruck and Saltzberg, instead of making our way direct from Venice to Vienna, and so on, by railroad, to the nearest point beyond, at which that road approaches Gräffenberg. Nor did even this content us. Having decided that we *must* revisit Innspruck and Saltzberg, we next called a council upon the propriety of going through the magnificent new pass recently opened by Austria, called the Pass of Ampezzo. The shorter way, I believe, would have been by the Val di Suzana to Trent, and so across the Brenner. But this we had done before, and only the preceding year, when returning to Florence from England, through Germany. So it was carried, *nem. con.*, that we should enter upon this magnificent gorge at Senavalle, and pass through it into the Pusterthal at Niederdorf, which enabled us to recover the great Brenner road a little above Brixen. Let no travellers under similar circumstances ever decide otherwise. It is scarcely possible, I think, for the imagination to conceive more stupendous mountain scenery than this road displays. Moreover, it is like all roads made by the Austrian government, (and to use a familiar form of praise,) as good as it is beautiful. A thousand studies of rock, wood, and water, such as would have made the heart of G. Poussin dance within him, might be found by artists on this road, and that without scrambling an inch out of it to find them. What they might meet with, if they did scramble a little, who shall say?

We passed within a very short distance—
two miles, I think—of the birth-place of Titian,
called Piave de Cadore.   The family of Ve-
cellio still exists there; and it was our purpose
to have made a pilgrimage to the spot, but
we were prevented doing so by a hard shower
of rain.   By the way, it is impossible for any
one at all familiar with the pictures of Titian
not to feel that the backgrounds, which even
in half-length portraits are so often, by means
of an open window, made to give such a magical charm to his pictures, have their originals
in this region.   I must not pause to prate
about Prague, only just observing, that those
seven castles belonging to the King of Bohemia,
of which our well-nigh forgotten Lawrence
Sterne makes honourable mention, are unquestionably to be found in this very grand city,
collected into one, and now known by the
name of the Ilrodschin.   It is said to contain
four hundred and forty rooms; and although
I cannot say that I entered them all, I can
truly aver that I have not the smallest doubt
of the fact.   If the number had been stated
as greater, I should have readily believed it

possible, from the enormous distance to which the almost endless edifice seems to extend itself. Amongst many other valuable things, it contains by far the finest ball-room I ever entered.

And now, being at Prague, we might have transported ourselves to Hohenstadt, a point at the distance of about twenty-eight English miles from Gräffenberg, right easily by railroad. But it was decreed by fate that we should discover that Dresden and its gallery were not only at an easy day's distance from Prague, but also that a part of the distance might be traversed by a steam-boat on the Elbe, a mode of travelling so exceedingly restorative to the limbs of way-worn travellers, that a very few minutes' consideration convinced us all that it would be a manifest want of common sense if we did not profit by it.

This, taken (of course) in conjunction with the undeniable fact that we should rather prefer seeing the picture-gallery at Dresden, than not, induced us to make a little farther delay, and to set off at four o'clock in the morning for the Saxon capital.

This excursion was, altogether, a most delightful one. What the Dresden picture gallery is, I need not trouble myself to mention; its *quite* unequalled treasures being rather too notorious for my doing so to be of any possible utility to any one. But, for the same reason which has led me to linger thus on my road to Gräffenberg, in order to point out how much its distance is shortened by the enchantments scattered along the road, I may just mention that we all agreed in thinking Dresden, even independent of its matchless pictures, one of the most *piacevole* and attractive cities we ever entered. Our little voyage, too, brought us within such short distance of the beautiful region called the Saxon Switzerland, as made us fully comprehend how well it deserved the name.

Late on the evening of the third day we re-entered Prague, and early on the following morning placed ourselves in one of the comfortable railroad carriages, (which, had we occupied it long enough, would have taken us to Vienna,) and felt at length pretty tolerably sure that we were actually going to Gräffenberg.

*   *   *   *   *

And now, my object being to make myself as useful as possible to all who may chance to follow me thither, I shall make no apologies for any minuteness of description into which I may chance to fall, feeling certain that the persons for whom these pages are chiefly intended, will thank me for it; for Gräffenberg is not only a great way from England, but it is very much out of the *common way*, in more senses than one, and I know by experience that all particulars concerning it may be useful.

On reaching Hohenstadt, there seemed to exist some doubt among the persons to whom we applied at the station, respecting the carriage that was to take us on, as to whether it was in truth the nearest point to Gräffenberg at which we could be set down; and we all, naturally, began to share these doubts when we discovered that no conveyance was to be found either at the station, or near it, that could convey us to the place of our destination. Very fortunately, however, a carriage capable of conveying our party arrived from Gräffenberg at the moment that our embarrassment seemed at its height; for the train had passed on, and we had just ascertained that there was little chance of our getting either lodging or food when it had left us.   An hour's bait enabled this welcome conveyance to set off again upon its return, but with the understanding that we were not to arrive at Gräffenberg that night, but must sleep at a little place called Huhndorf, about half way.

We were too glad to obtain a conveyance upon any conditions to dispute the point with the driver, although at four o'clock on a Mid-summer day there seemed no danger of being benighted, even if we had decided upon going the whole of the twenty-seven miles without pausing for the night, midway.   But notwith-standing this rather discouraging description of the Hohenstadt station, as the point from which to leave the railroad for Gräffenberg, it *is* the best.   The Gräffenberg post is carried to Vienna by a stage-coach, and meets the train at Olmütz; but the distance to Olmütz is nearly double that to Hohenstadt.

Our night's lodging at Huhndorf was at one

of those wild-looking farm-house inns which are so frequently found in the remoter provinces of the Austrian empire. A snug stay-at-home English reader would shudder were I to rehearse *all* the particulars of the *accommodation* we met with—but we got abundance of good white bread and milk, and the three ladies of the party lay down in their three narrow wooden troughs, (for so only can I describe the bedsteads,) in one room, as contentedly as they could. Upon this occasion, as well as upon one or two others, while traversing Bohemia, my Italian man-servant had to watch his bed deliberately constructed before his eyes from straw brought from the farm-yard, and reduced to seemly shape by the help of a pitchfork. For this species of bed we repeatedly paid very nearly as much as for our own; but there was no means of mending the matter, for our four beds generally took every pillow and mattress in the house.

On at length reaching the end of our journey, we found that lodging ourselves at *Gräffenberg* was out of the question. The hamlet so called, and in which the establishment of

Dr. Preissnitz is situated, stands upon the summit of a high and very steep hill, and consists almost entirely of a few miserable cottages, of which one portion is let for lodgings, and the other inhabited by cows. We had been strongly advised not to go into Dr. Preissnitz's house, as, from its receiving some hundreds of patients afflicted by pretty nearly all the ills of humanity, it was not likely to afford an agreeable residence.

On first arriving, we took up our quarters at the Gräffenberg Hotel, in the little town at the foot of the hill called Freiwalden. We had been told this was the best, and, as far as I have been able to discover, it is the only hotel in the place, and to travellers as way-worn as ourselves it appeared almost comfortable. A very few hours passed in Freiwalden sufficed to obtain as much information as was necessary to convince us that, though we were come to Gräffenberg, it was at Freiwalden that we must lodge. Nevertheless, my son climbed the hill before he could consent to our taking apartments at the foot of it, but speedily returned to tell us that so it must be, as our attempting to get into any of the places at Gräffenberg was out of the question.

Except the large mansion of the wealthy Burgomeister, I doubt if there be a single house in Freiwalden which does not let lodgings, and as the place is long, and straggling, there are a great many of them. A short search enabled us to judge what sort of accommodation was to be expected, and we found several, still unoccupied, which seemed capable of accommodating us tolerably well, and from among these we selected the best. And now we thought we were settled, and that we had nothing more to do than order our various trunks to be conveyed from the inn, and to take possession.

But here we were most grievously mistaken. I never remember to have witnessed a more grotesque distress than that which fell upon us when we proclaimed to our landlord that it was our intention immediately to take possession. We then learned, with what feelings of dismay let those who are seeking rest after a thousand miles of wandering imagine, that before we could sleep in the lodgings we must either buy or hire beds, bolsters, pillows, blankets, and counterpanes; and that before we could eat in them, we must buy plates, dishes, cups, glasses, &c. &c. &c.—not to mention the whole *batterie de cuisine.*

This information seemed to throw us into a situation infinitely worse than if we had found no lodgings at all, for then we should have made up our minds to remain at the queer little hotel, and there would have been an end of it.   What was to be done?   Had we been a hundred instead of a thousand miles from Florence, I certainly think I should have shown a white feather, and have gently hinted at the probable advantages of going home again. But, as it was, despair gave me courage, as it has done others before me.

> " Returning were as tedious as go o'er ;"

and therefore we, one and all, meekly set to work, to make the best we could of our condition.

Certainly there are some few of our distant friends who would have felt inclined to laugh at us, could they have witnessed the scene which followed. There we all stood together, in the little shop which professes to have everything that man, in his domestic state, requires. But this boast should be understood with a difference; it can only mean to refer to the wants of man in the first stage of civilization. There we stood, however, endeavouring, one and all of us, to remember all the things that were absolutely necessary to existence, and this went on till the whole counter was covered from end to end with crockery of all sorts, and a lot of coarse pottery, by way of crocks, kettles, and *casseroles*. Fortunately for our purses, this simple sort of fitting up cost wonderfully little, and when at length the unexpected work was done, and we got at last into our humble dwelling, we all seemed as proud of having a salt-cellar and a cream-jug, &c. &c., as if they had all been of burnished gold.

Then came the requesting a visit from the great doctor, and great was the interest with which we looked at him. His simplicity of manner is still that of a friendly, kind-hearted peasant, but his brow and the expression of his mouth show intellect and resolution. I am assured that he still reads with great difficulty, and that he cannot write at all. The examination of his two patients produced a series of directions which, in the first instance, are, I believe, pretty similar in all cases. They were both to live with wet towels round the waist; both to be enfolded twice or thrice a day in a wet sheet; both to lessen their ordinary quantity of warm garments; both to drink about a dozen large glasses of water per diem; and both to abstain from tea, coffee, wine, and fermented beverages of all sorts.

In addition to this, and to be adopted more gradually by the lady than by the gentleman, a cold bath was ordered, sometimes for the whole person, sometimes for sitting in; and, moreover, the most mysterious process of all, consisting of the being closely rolled up in a wet sheet, and then enveloped over it in a blanket of enormous thickness. This process is technically called "*packing*," and, by what I hear, well deserves the name. The patient lies thus packed for about twenty minutes on the bed, and the sensation is described by some as being very delightful. At the end of the twenty minutes he is plunged in a cold bath. After every application of water, a brisk, short walk is prescribed *de rigueur*, and long walks, both morning and evening, into the bargain.

The gentleman has a bath-man, and the lady a bath-woman, to attend upon them, whose duty it is, in addition to preparing the baths, wet sheets, dry blankets, and so forth, to rub their patients very perseveringly with the hand while they are enveloped in the wet sheet. After a few days of this initiatory practice, the *douche* is applied with more or less severity, according to the strength and condition of the patient. And this, as far as I can understand it, is all.

The skill of Dr. Preissnitz is, however, highly necessary in all critical cases, to regulate the degree in which these different operations are to be administered; and the statements which meet us from all quarters, of the wonderful acuteness with which he discerns the peculiarities of constitution or disease, are most extraordinary, and inspire, as they ought to do, the most unbounded confidence in all who place themselves in his hands.

So many particular cases have already been laid before the public, in which this most natural, though hitherto neglected remedy, has produced effects that, in some instances, almost appear miraculous, that the reduplication of them must be superfluous. The company here, amounting to many hundred persons, meet together freely, and acquaintances are easily and readily made. The great advantage of this is, that one is enabled to hear in detail a multitude of cases, which, by their irresistible force of evidence, leaves no *possibility* of doubt upon the mind respecting the truth of all the most important facts which have been laid before the public respecting the power of this long-neglected agent upon the human frame. I am far from thinking, however, that a journey to Gräffenberg is necessary for its application. I speak not now of the notorious fact, that there are many other establishments of a similar kind, but of the more important one still, that, as a constant and sure remedy in the great majority of maladies to which the human race is subject, it may be applied as safely, and almost as easily, as the washing our hands. It must never be forgotten, however, that the acute philosopher of Gräffenberg by no means rests upon the application of water alone as a means of cure. This is his most active agent; but he has other agents also, which are scarcely, if at all, less important. The total and entire abstraction of all viands, all beverages, all habits, all indulgences, hostile in the very least degree to the healthy, that is to say, the *natural* state of man, is enforced as a condition upon every patient, and, unless complied with to the very fullest extent, Dr. Preissnitz ceases his attendance.

A little reflection upon the *amount of power*, independent of his watery applications, which this invests him with, may perhaps lessen the incredulity which many persons still avow on the subject of the Gräffenberg cures. In order fully to feel this, it may perhaps be necessary, in the present state of the world, to come to Gräffenberg, for there only, I imagine, can the contrast between the mode of existence upon

which he insists, and that ordinarily led by
what are called civilized human beings, be
fairly appreciated.

In London, Paris, or any of the great capitals of Europe, the division and occupation of
the day is, for the most part, very similar, as
far as the habits influential on the constitution
are concerned. In this estimate I would not
include any whose habits were grossly profli-
gate or intemperate, but only such as follow
with the ordinary degree of moderation the
customs and manners of those around them.
Let us trace the history of a London lady's
day, as far as her health is concerned. Let
her be of the middle class, middle age, and
middle place in the scale of intellect.

She rises about nine: the first thing she
does on quitting her bed is to enwrap herself
in a dressing-gown, probably of some soft,
clinging material, which effectually impedes
the approach of air to her person. She then
gently applies a very moderate quantity of water,
generally warm, to such portions of her skin
as she thinks necessary. This varies a good
deal, I believe, in different individuals, but

entire immersion is the daily habit of very few. The process of dressing need not be dwelt upon, excepting indeed to observe that not above one woman in a hundred completes her toilet without materially impeding the most important of all the vital actions, namely, that of breathing. Then comes the breakfast, at which it is generally found necessary to excite the appetite by some article of pungent flavour, either sweet, salt, or savoury, whether digestible or not, it is not very customary to consider, accompanying it by either hot tea, or coffee; and then follows, in the great majority of cases, many sedentary hours, which, however well employed they may be, in other respects, have very rarely the preservation of health for their object. And then the ladies go to luncheon. This meal varies considerably in different families; but let *all* English ladies ask themselves whether they do not think this meal rather a more generous one than the preservation of health requires?

Now comes the time for exercise, to such as do not prefer sitting at home to receive visits instead, and they go out, either to walk a little, drive a little, or, some few of them, to ride a little, and then they come home a good deal tired, for they have probably talked, and perhaps *shopped* with considerable energy; and, till the hour of dressing for dinner, they either lie upon a sofa, or sit deep sunk in a well-stuffed arm-chair.

Dinner is the next scene, and that too, as we all know, varies prodigiously. But of all the ladies in London who sit down to dinner, how many are there who are regulated in their choice of what they eat, solely by the consideration of what is wholesome? And they take wine; little, or much, but they all take wine— and afterwards, the greater number take also a cup of strong hot coffee.

At about an hour before midnight, that portion of our countrywomen who are happy enough to "move in good society" have probably finished the important and rather fatiguing task of dressing themselves for the fourth time, and, having taken a little hot tea, they set forth to spend two or three hours, or it may be many more, in a highly heated atmosphere, composed in some degree, certainly, of the material necessary to the process of breathing, but mingled with a variety of exhalations which need not be analysed, in order to convince us, after a little experience, that the human lungs might find themselves more completely at ease without them; and after taking a little ice, and, it may be, a little champagne, they come home and go to bed in a room that their faithful servants have made as close as possible, and, after the slight use of a little more warm water, they lie down and sleep as long as they can.

Now, then, let us take one of these ladies' and place her at Gräffenberg. I will in no way exaggerate any of the features of the life she leads there, but only observe, that if she be a patient of Dr. Preissnitz, no choice is allowed her. The example I will take, shall be a person of the same class, age, and condition, as before, and I will not suppose her to be afflicted by any worse complaint than what is pretty sure to overtake, in a greater or less degree, every one who has led, from early youth to middle age, such a life as I have been describing.

Having achieved the journey, settled herself

in her lodging, seen the doctor, and hired her bath-woman, she will go on as follows.

She will get out of bed at four o'clock, A.M., and be immediately enveloped by her attendant in a sheet that has been dipped into fresh cold water, which has been wrung from it just sufficiently to prevent its running about her in streams. This wet sheet is wrapped closely round her, and the bath-woman rubs her briskly on the outside of it, with both her hands, the patient herself being also enjoined to rub herself in the same manner, as actively as possible. The lady is then left to herself, and employs a few moments in fanning her wet person with the sheet, the room being made to receive the while as much fresh air as possible, and the moisture upon her skin dries so rapidly during this process, that very little subsequent wiping is necessary. The bath-woman then wraps a thick wet cloth about three yards long round her waist, and another over it, of the same texture and dimensions, but dry. This is the only stay she is permitted to wear. She is strongly recommended to wear no stockings . . . The flannel garment

usually worn by English women is strictly forbidden, and as light a petticoat and gown as
can be procured, form her whole dress.

Having invested herself with all rapidity in
this, (no combing and brushing of the hair
can take place till afterwards,) she sallies
forth, with a light sun-bonnet on her head,
and a drinking-glass in her hand. She walks
briskly to a cold fresh spring, fills her glass
once, twice, thrice, perhaps, and swallows the
limpid contents. She then mounts, at her best
speed, some of the steep hills which surround
the place, and whenever she meets with a font
by the way, she stops, fills her ever-ready glass,
and drinks.

This walking must continue till eight o'clock,
when she returns to breakfast, carefully made
ready—for, trust me, she is furiously hungry—
and finds black or brown bread, (if she can eat
it, but if not, she is indulged with white,) a huge
jug of fresh milk, butter *à discrétion*, and as
many of the delicious wild strawberries that
are native here as she can eat. At nine she is
again enveloped in a wet sheet, and the moisture of her bandage is renewed, and then she

is recommended to lie down and go to sleep; and I have heard, as yet, of no insomnolency obstinate enough to resist this prescription. The sleep is sound, quiet, and most deliciously refreshing. On awaking from this sleep, it is, if I mistake not, in the common order of the day's work to take what is called the packed, or sweating bath; but, of course, the applications vary according to individual cases.

The packing process consists in being rolled in a wet sheet, and very tightly enveloped in a very thick blanket over it. You are then left to lie bound, hands and feet, for about twenty minutes, and perspiration more or less copious generally ensues. The patient is then unbound, and plunged into a cold bath, and then sent to walk for half an hour, but is forbidden to walk in the sun. The douche, which is the severest of all the applications of cold water, and which is not at once administered to persons unused to this sort of discipline, is usually given after the packing.

All this pretty well occupies the time till one o'clock, at which hour every body dines. " Sancho's dread doctor and his wand" are *not*

there, excepting, indeed, at the side-board.
No beverage but water is permitted; but, with
the exception of soup, I cannot find that any
viands are forbidden; and the great physician
seems, I think, to pride himself upon the perfectly healthy powers of digestion which his
system produces. His resolute forbiddance of
soup is not from any danger of its being rich,
but he permits not the introduction of any
warm fluid into the stomach.

After dinner, the patients may sleep again
if they want it, or if they prefer walking they
may walk, provided always that they do not
walk in sunshine. At four, another wet sheet
is administered, followed by a newly wetted
bandage; and then they walk again, and amuse
themselves if they like by seeking some of the
daily dozen of glasses of water which they
are enjoined to drink, at more distant springs;
but at seven, they must return to eat—the
materials of the meal being the same as at
breakfast; and after this they are recommended to climb more hills for an hour or
two.

At ten, as far as I am able to judge, every

body goes to bed, and that all those subjected to the treatment are ready for it, is by no means surprising, for it is certainly very fatiguing. But the fatigue is of a nature that appears to ensure the most delightful sleep to all who endure it.

Is not this statement sufficient to prove that Dr. Preissnitz assumes and exercises more power over his patients than the mere use of cold water can give him? No one that has ever taken a cold bath, either in river or sea, but must have been aware that the immersion produced a very powerful, and, generally, a very delightful sensation, and that it is likely to produce very decided effects upon the health. But I know no one, excepting among the patients of Dr. Preissnitz, who has been induced to break through all the artificial habits of social life, in order to try if he might not feel better if he abandoned himself to the agency of air, water, exercise, and sleep, instead.

I am far, however, from meaning to say that I consider the superintending watchfulness of such an acute and experienced experimentalist as Dr. Preissnitz, as of no value.

All that I have heard of his practice here, convinces me of the contrary; and had I a friend afflicted by any chronic complaint of long standing, or suffering from the effects of any paralytic affection, or, in short, from any other infirmity of a nature either alarming or doubtful, I would certainly, *were it possible*, have him transported to Freiwalden, and placed under the care of Dr. Preissnitz. But as the transporting a sick man to a place so remote from the greater part of Europe as Freiwalden in Silesia, can never be an easy, and may often be an impossible task, I have dwelt upon such parts of the Gräffenberg curative process as I conceive might be practised at home.

The result of all I have seen and heard of Dr. Preissnitz and his practice, has been to inspire me not only with deep respect, but most sincere admiration also.

First the comforting, and then the healing, qualities of cold water, " were borne in upon the mind" of Dr. Preissnitz, while he was himself suffering from the effects of a severe accident. He was then quite a youth, but appears at once to have been struck by the importance of the discovery he had made. When a man is thoroughly convinced of a truth, and earnestly desirous of propagating it, he generally grows eloquent; and among his friends and equals, (the peasants of Gräffenberg and Freiwalden,) Dr. Preissnitz obtained sufficient influence to make many of them submit to his discipline. By degrees his curative attempts became sufficiently famous to attract the attention of the curé of the parish; and the good man thought it his duty to denounce from the pulpit a system that owed its invention either to fraud or folly, and its success to ignorance and credulity.

His cures went on, however, notwithstanding.

At length the curé himself fell sick of a violent fever, and was given over by three physicians, who had been summoned from different parts of the country to attend him, and the last religious consolations were bestowed on him. After this awful ceremony was ended, and his reverend confessor departed, the curé despatched a messenger to the house of the peasant Preissnitz, requesting his attendance. He came, and the dying curé asked him if he thought he could save him. Preissnitz declared himself ready to try; and in a marvellously short time the patient was well enough to address to his parishioners, from the pulpit, a recantation of all his errors on the subject of cold water. The good curé is still alive and in excellent health, and has ever since been one of the most strenuous advocates of the system, and also one of the most cordial friends of the inventor. This was the first patient he ever had above the rank of a peasant.

But things are greatly changed with him now. Last year the Archduke François Charles, heir presumptive to the imperial throne of Austria, paid him a most flattering visit. Those who witnessed the meeting, declare it to have been extremely interesting. The Archduke's first words, as he cordially extended his hand to the rustic philosopher, were, " There is but one Preissnitz;" while the man of conscious genius received it, not without emotion—far from it—but with a sort

of modest composure, equally remote both from
audacity and shyness, and which seemed to
show an equally just appreciation of his illus-
trious visitant and of himself.   This year the
Emperor has commanded that a medal should
be struck in his honour; and we were fortunate enough to be at Gräffenberg the day on
which the Governor of Silesia presented it to
him.   This ceremony took place in the Town
Hall, and high mass was afterwards performed
in the church upon the occasion.   In the
evening a ball was given by the doctor to *all*
his patients; the fine, or, at least, the finest
folks, being received in the great dining-room
of the establishment, and the humbler division
of the company in another large room in a
different part of the building.   The good doctor looked very gay and very happy; and his
broad gold medal, suspended by a red ribbon,
was gazed at with applause by (*on dit*) above
five hundred persons.   He has a nice-looking,
quiet-mannered little wife, and six daughters;
the eldest a pretty-looking girl, about eighteen.
It is said that he very deeply regrets the not
having a son, to whom he might impart the

experience of his life, and his inferences from it. We are assured that there is no person upon whom he has, as yet, bestowed this valuable confidence; but that, on the contrary, he is by no means communicative on the subject to those who have endeavoured to lead him to converse upon it.

Nevertheless, he is said to have been heard repeatedly to express regret that his system must die with him, because he knew no one who would be capable of carrying it on.

In my opinion, very great and universal benefit might be derived from the visits of intelligent, (*and if possible*) unprejudiced, professional men of all countries, to the spot. They must, of course, be able to speak German; and if intelligent questioners, and intelligent lookers-on, for a year or two, I am greatly inclined to think that they would be able to carry away all that it was important they should know. Nobody living can be further than I am from wishing to deny that Preissnitz is a man of genius; but I do not feel it possible to conceive that he can, correctly speaking, be termed a man of science. That he has carefully obtained the result of many ingenious experiments, cannot be doubted; and this is knowledge, to a certain extent. He is not now, I believe, much above fifty years old, and he may, and I trust he will, go on,

> " Till old experience doth attain
>   To something of prophetic vein."

But even this cannot strictly deserve the name of science, as we have been accustomed to hear it used. He knows that, under certain circumstances, if he does so and so, such and such will be the results; but as to the why and the wherefore, I suspect he neither knows, nor has sought, by help of instruction, to know much. He can write his own name, they say, fairly and clearly, but beyond this he does not use his pen—keeping a secretary, who receives and answers all letters for him.

It is said, too, that he reads, but *not with facility;* education having been, during his younger days, much less advanced among the subjects of the Austrian empire than it is at present. And thus knowledge is—

> ——— " at one entrance,"

and that a most important one—" quite shut out." He reasons, I am told, when undertaking to defend (not to *explain*, for that he never does) his system; but it is not, by what I hear, in a very scientific vein. For instance, I am told, that when particularly expansive, he has said, " Providence gives us nothing that is not necessary to us. Why do streams of fresh clear water flow so copiously over the earth?" I perfectly agree with him in his proposition, and so do many wiser folks; and when the world is a little older, it will probably become more generally of the same opinion than it is at present; but, nevertheless, this sort of reasoning will not make a safe physician, as might easily be proved by pushing the same sort of argument in different directions.

I believe Preissnitz to be a WONDERFULLY clever man, and I think he has made a great hit. Woe to mankind, if there be no men of science to be found, with minds sufficiently eager to receive all knowledge, to make them seize upon it, let it come whence, and how it may! Accident has led to the discovery of some of the most useful mysteries of nature known to man; and what matters it whether the accident happen to a Silesian peasant or to a doctor of medicine?

That the application of cold water, in various ways, to the human body DOES produce effects which were never dreamed of till the experiments of Preissnitz led to their discovery, is already much too well known for any man to contradict with impunity. It may, indeed, be possible to collect a few profoundly ignorant individuals in a corner, who might listen to such doubts without laughing at the man who uttered them; but no one can go forth into the world with such wilful falsehood, or benighted ignorance, on his lips, without meeting the reward he merits. This state of things the discoverer has lived to see; but we may be very sure that much remains behind, which his destined day of life will not be long enough to show him. When the strength and applicability of steam was first hit upon, who guessed that it would, in a few years, enable all the world to traverse earth and ocean?

But the powers and principalities, the scientific bodies, and the learned associations, above all the physicians of the earth (not the druggists, "*bien entendu*,") will do greatly less than their duty if they permit Preissnitz to die before they have taken care that trustworthy eye-witnesses have been placed in a condition to report what he is doing.

The only reasonable opposition which I can imagine to the careful examination of this system must come from the compounders and dispensers of drugs; for so completely has the Gräffenberg sage thrown physic to the dogs, that I already feel, though not one of his patients, that I shall never again be induced to take a dose till I have first tried the effect of a few glasses of cold water.

But were such learned deputations as I have alluded to, sent hither for the purpose of testing the value of the experiments going on, I own I think they would have one great difficulty to contend with, and that no less a one than the danger of not preserving their gravity, while engaged upon an inquiry of the very gravest kind.

But let me not be misunderstood. So far from

thinking any one of these experiments a subject of mockery, I almost doubt whether any
other experiments are going on at this hour
in any part of the world, relative to natural
science, which I could feel to be of as great
importance to the human race. Oh, no! It
is not the prescriptions or the experiments of
Dr. Preissnitz which would provoke the mirth
I speak of, but the incredibly grotesque style
in which the various patients set themselves to
profit by the cure they have come so far to
seek.

These patients are collected from pretty
nearly all the nations of the earth; and these
new and startling prescriptions are likely
enough to affect the imagination, and even the
practical common sense, differently in different
cases.

We have here, at this moment, Austrians,
Bavarians, Bohemians, Silesians, Hungarians,
Prussians, Lombards, Sardinians, Romans,
Tuscans, Spaniards, Poles, Russians, Turks,
French, Americans, and—need I add—ENGLISH,
(in much greater numbers than the natives of
any other country, unless all who boast the

German language as their mother tongue are
to be accounted one people.)

It must not be supposed, however, that this
grotesqueness, in the general effect produced
by the Gräffenberg and Freiwalden company,
is occasioned by any striking differences of
national costume; *that* is wholly and entirely
lost sight of, in general obedience to the orders
of the great physician; but the sort of universal licence and individual whim which this
prescribed abdication of ordinary dress leads
to must really be seen to be believed.   To
account for this, it must be remembered, that
the great majority of the company consists of
persons who have left their homes, and con-
sented to relinquish all the usual comforts of
life, in the hope of recovering or improving
their health.   This object, for the time being,
is very rationally the paramount purpose and
occupation of their existence—all minor considerations, such as conformity to the fashion
of the day, or even to the ordinary style of
appearance usually adopted by persons of their
age, country, class, and condition, are wholly
set aside, and if not actually forgotten, are

only remembered as furnishing an amusing contrast with their present entire freedom from all such restraint.

Then come the fun and fancy, dictated by whim, liberty, and high spirits—for somehow or other, despite the entire absence of all ordinary sources of amusement, the great majority of the patients do appear to be in very high spirits—and this fun and fancy display themselves in exaggerating the prescriptions of the doctor as to light clothing. The appearance of the men, gentle and simple, has something so wild in it, that even yet I can scarcely get over my first impression, that they are persons escaped from a lunatic asylum.

Not only are they without cravats, but with their collars and the breasts of the shirts thrown wide open, as if a panting necessity for air at every pore compelled them to abandon all thoughts of common decency. No gloves are on their hands, no stockings on their legs, no hats on their heads; no coats, no waistcoats, have they, but for the most part a sort of coarse-looking garment, made more like a little short carter's frock than any-

thing else which I can recollect, to compare it
to. Sometimes this is of one colour, and
sometimes of another, but generally varying
between the ordinary hue of a Cumberland
maud, and a tint as pale as that of brown
holland. The open shirt that is displayed
under this is sometimes white, but much
oftener coloured. The hair (not, indeed, the
beard; that seems always left to grow *à discretion*) is cut as short as that of a convict.

In addition to all this, the pace at which
they walk, nay, every movement they make,
seems propelled by a preternatural degree of
activity, and there is often a bright freshness
of complexion observable, that suggests the
idea of a vigorous state of body and a rapid
circulation of blood. This describes the general appearance of the male part of the company
whenever you meet them; but by resorting to
the most frequented paths, at the hours of the
principal water exercises, you are sure to encounter a multitude of men and women, who,
in conformity to the discipline enjoined, are
straining every nerve to assist the effects of
the remedy by active movement; and it is

then, most especially, that the majority of
those you meet, especially of the male sex,
have the air of having escaped from their
keepers.

In that charming, but almost forgotten
little volume, entitled " The Miseries of Human
Life," there is a scene descriptive of the agony
of zeal with which dancers who have just indulged in taking an ice, rush onward through
the dance, in the hope of preventing any danger
from it, and exclaiming as they go—" Hands
across, for the love of mercy! Down the
middle, in the name of Heaven!" Now, though
the ladies and gentlemen of Gräffenberg and
Freiwalden who have just taken their douche,
or their sitting bath, or their wet sheet, do
not thus exclaim, it is impossible not to read
the same object and the same anxiety in their
eyes and gestures ; and even if the selfish fear
of being knocked down did not cause one to
step aside, I really hope that we should take
care not to occasion the delay of a quarter of
a second in their course, from mere humanity.

As to the dress of the ladies, it is much less
remarkable than that of the gentlemen.   The

" Gräffenberg stockings," which is the phrase
in use for describing the wearing no stockings
at all, being the most remarkable visible feature of it; but when we recollect that they
are all a petticoat *minus*, and that, instead of
a corset, they have three yards of wet linen
twisted round them, we cannot be much surprised if, somehow or other, they do not altogether look like " folks of this world."

An observation was made to me the other
day by a gentleman who has been for many
months an inmate of the Gräffenberg establishment, containing, as we are told, above two
hundred patients, which struck me as important. This gentleman is a military man, long
in active service, and therefore long accustomed to living among large assemblies of men,
and in the habit of constant intercourse with
them; but never, he said, had he seen so many
human beings thrown together whose tempers
seemed so uniformly even and amiable.—
" There are in that house," said he, " persons
suffering under almost every imaginable kind
of disease, yet they are always good-humoured,
always cheerful."

If this be so, and I have every reason in the world for believing that he spoke the truth, the observation is as much in favour of the water cure, as any that I remember to have heard.

Gräffenberg, July 13*th*, 1846.

THE VALHALLA.

THE VALHALLA.

THERE are, I believe, many persons besides myself who, hoping to improve their health, or increase their enjoyment, take the trouble of exchanging the climate of their native England for the brighter one of Italy, every winter; and to such, a few hints as to the manner in which this may be done with the least annoyance may be useful.

Somebody—I cannot remember who, where, or when, has pithily exclaimed, "I would rather be d——d than pitied." Without going quite so far as this energetic personage, I am ready to confess that, in moderation, I share the feeling, and therefore that I have been occasionally vexed in spirit by the compassion expressed for me by sundry of my friends, and acquaintance, on account of the tedious, troublesome turmoil of travelling, which I yearly inflict on myself by my passings and repassings of the rocky barrier, which so many contemplate from youth to age in their mind's eye, without ever venturing to traverse once.

Let me assure them, in the consolatory words of Prospero, that they may " tell their piteous hearts there's no harm done."

I am quite ready to confess, however, that did I pack myself up twice a year, with every faculty locked up like the contents of my travelling trunk, save only that of consciousness that I was in the act of rolling along, my condition would not only be indeed pitiable, but my conviction that it was so such as to ensure my gratitude to all who would bestow a sigh upon my sufferings. But I manage better than that; and although my migrations have of late years been as faithful as those of the swallow, and the terminus of each transit more precisely the same than we have any good right to proclaim his to be, yet I have contrived to make almost as many picturesque tours, and for the most part various too, as I have made journeys, so that the recollections of these pitied journeyings are among the most delightful of my existence.

"La belle France!" Our gay-tempered neighbours have appropriated this pleasant epithet so long and so steadily, that it now really seems to belong to them by right, and that one should be guilty of as much injustice as incivility in disputing their claim to it. In truth, if they would be contented to accept as true the often-made assertion that PARIS was FRANCE, nobody perhaps would feel inclined to dispute the point, for it is very certain that, in its way, Paris is one of the most beautiful cities in the world. It is neither so immense, nor so redolent of wealth as London; nor so poetically interesting as Florence; nor so venerable as Rome; nor so bright as Naples; but it is beautiful—gaily, splendidly, and variously beautiful—and I, in my turn, should be seized with a compassionate fit, did I meet with any one incapable of enjoying—ay, and keenly, too—the graceful vagaries of its mosaic embellishments.

But, having once heroically made up your mind to drive through the barrier, leaving the famous walls, and all the pretty glittering things contained within them, behind you, I must candidly confess that, in my opinion, you leave most of the beauty of " la belle France" behind you also.   In fact, considering the great extent, and the good clear atmosphere of the country, it is quite extraordinary that there should be so little in France (out of Paris) which is likely to check the speed of a passing traveller.

The churches, some few of them at least, make an exception; but as to scenery, there is scarcely a single county in our little empire of islands, that might not show spots of greater picturesque beauty than the whole the broad " belle France" could furnish throughout her whole enormous territory.   Even the fine old towns, of which there are very many deserving the close attention of the learned antiquary, are, for the most part, so much less striking as to picturesque effect than those of Flanders and Germany, that they rarely suggest themselves to the memory of persons familiar

with these latter, as specimens of this peculiar
species of beauty.

In truth, the long leagues of France con-
stitute " the rub" of an English traveller's
journey to Italy; but railroads are becoming
every day more and more epidemic, and France,
though of late she seems to have been too deeply
occupied by her celebrated specimen of Chinese
rivalry in the wall line, to pay much attention
to any other great national work, appears now to
have conceived projects of locomotiveness com-
mensurate with her greatness, and I heartily
hope, for my own particular convenience, as
well as for that of a few scores of millions of
other people, that no symptoms of visionary
delusion such as have been observed to attend
other epidemic attacks, will be found to have
mixed themselves with her schemes.   The very
idea of a railroad from Calais to Marseilles has
something of magical luxury in it, which those
only can fully appreciate who have known what
it is, over and over again, to traverse the same
space, not at railroad speed, but at that of
French horses.

But although the French, like a magnificent

nation as they are, know how to do great things greatly, they cannot be expected to lay down this line of about six hundred and fifty miles without some little delay, and therefore those whose journeyings southward cannot wait till it is finished may find it useful to meditate before they set out, on the best methods of beguiling this wondrously wearisome journey, or else of completely changing their route, and so lessening their fatigue, even while lengthening the distance.

In passing from England to Italy, I have usually endeavoured to lay in a stock of good humour at Paris, by passing a few days there, en route, and then, desperately dragging myself at one long pull to Lyons, have sought and found my reward by diverging from thence, sometimes in one direction, and sometimes in another, so as to enjoy each year a different excursion of the very highest picturesque beauty, without very greatly adding to the distance which was still to be traversed before we arrived at our winter moorings in Florence.

But this year we contrived to cut "la belle France" altogether, and by means of steam by

land and by water, managed so as to reach
Florence without having placed a foot on the
oft traversed soil, " *dove se dicono*, OUI." From
Darlington to London, I travelled at the delicious pace of fifty miles an hour, and proceeded,
after a day or two of lingering in the Great
Babylon, to Dover by railroad, to Ostend by
steam boat, and thence again, by aid of the same
vapoury, yet constant friend, to Cologne. This
latter division of the smoothly-gliding process
however, was not performed at the rate of fifty
miles an hour. But it was very well for a beginning, and a marvellously great improve-
ment upon the pace at which I had last reached
the venerable city, glorious by the visitation
of eleven thousand virgins in one charming
group, *as well* as by its position on the most
beautiful river in Europe, and its possession
of a Dom Kirke which by the grandeur of its
conception may rival—nay, perhaps excel—
all the churches in the world except St. Peter's.

The church and the river together go far towards atoning for this *rather* acute angle on the
road to Italy; but when it is considered that most
people, besides the ordinary migration from a

summer to a winter residence, count it not a
sin to enjoy yearly a little fine-weather tour-
ing, the *coming round through Germany*
cannot be considered as *going out of the way*
to enjoy what you may find on the route.
This majestic minster itself is quite sufficient
to make such a deviation from the direct road
across "la belle France" extremely reasonable,
particularly at the present moment, when the
truly kingly king of Prussia is employing some
hundreds of workmen to complete the beautiful and stupendous work. And truly the king
"takes up the wondrous tale" in a manner
that makes one heartily hope he may live to
bring it to a conclusion.

And then the river!

Though I now navigated its "abounding"
waters for the seventh time, and had contemplated, since my first visit, the Rhone, the
Danube, and the Po, the lovely Rhine had lost
none of its charms for me; and as I stood,
despite of all imaginable obstacles, at the very
extremest point of the vessel's pointed head, I
thought that the successive pictures that I
came upon might vie in beauty with *almost*

any lake or river scenery that I had ever been happy enough to gaze upon.

At Mayence, I left the river, and reached Francfort by a commodious little railroad which brought us to the busy and brilliant free city with very laudable celerity; and then, excepting for the few miles between Bamberg and Nuremberg, I bade adieu to railroad speed, and for the rest of my journey sought enjoyment from lingering amidst ' what was beautiful.

At Wertzberg, I passed a day in prying into old churches, and so forth, and from the fort upon the hill, looked down upon one of the royal residences of Lewis of Bavaria, which was rendered interesting by my being told that our gracious Queen had passed a night there in the course of the preceding week. At Bamberg I was met by my son, and we enjoyed together a week's visit at the magnificent château of Seerhof, formerly the residence of the Prince Bishop of Bamberg, but now the property of the Baroness de Z——. Whilst there we gave a day to the antiquities of Bamberg,—and a fine old town it is. The cathedral, which has been recently, and like all King Lewis's works, well repaired, is a very noble edifice. From Bamberg to Nuremberg we once more fled for a few minutes along a rail; but having reached that venerable museum of gable ends and oriel windows, we were well contented to remain stationary for a while, in order to examine at leisure what is, I believe, allowed to be the most perfect specimen extant of a gothic mediæval city.

It is interesting to mark the distinctive national features of different lands when they are as strongly pronounced as between Germany and Italy. The sober, sturdy, steady, look of the German people, when contemplated after long familiarity with Italy, speaks in a language difficult to be misunderstood, and furnishes a sort of philosophical commentary on the history of both countries, which has great eloquence.

Not many months before, I found myself in the great church-yard of St. John at Nuremberg, I had stood gazing down from the Bologna road upon the Campo Santo of Florence. The Italian receptacle for the mortal relics of the Florentine citizens offered

to the eye little or nothing, save a large square
enclosure of coarse grass, with a lofty cross in
the midst of it and a very unconspicuous little
building on the one side, which served for a
chapel, from the shelter of which the officiating
priest utters the last short, and by no means
very solemn, valedictory blessing of the Romish
church.

"But where are the tombs?" I demanded
of a companion who stood beside me.

"There are none," he replied. "Tombs,
excepting when erected as objects of ostenta-
tion and magnificence for the gratification of
the living, or as loudly-demanded records of
some species of departed greatness, in honour
of the mighty dead, are not deemed necessary
in Italy. In the enclosure that you are looking
down upon are three hundred and sixty-five
pits, sunk deep into the earth. The stone
which covers the entrance to each is level with
the surface, and invisible except on close examination. One of these pits is opened at
midnight every night of the year in succession, and every night of the year the dead of
Florence are precipitated *coffinless* into the

abyss, which is then closed up again till the anniversary of the same hour on the following year."

" Oblivion indeed !" said I.

" Yes," he replied. " Excepting under peculiar circumstances, oblivion follows death more quickly under the bright skies of the sunny south, than amidst the more meditative, shadowy regions of the north. It should seem that where life is more keenly felt, death is more easily forgotten. The fables and legends of Italy may generally be traced to the life-like immortalities of the Pantheon, while those of the northern nations are for the most part furnished from the shadowy world of departed spirits. In Italy, if no halo of fame gleams with poetic light upon the dead, all traces of their past existence seem by common consent to be voted unseemly; and, instead of storied tombs to mark the spot where their forefathers sleep, the life-teeming survivors prefer consigning them to the undistinguishable abode that looks so unmeaningly smooth and vacant beneath us. If you will visit the old cities of Germany, you will find there burying grounds offering a very different picture of the national mind."

This conversation flashed across my memory as I stood amidst the venerable tombs of Nuremberg. In this crowded and most curious receptacle, every object I looked at seemed to indicate a ceaseless struggle with Time, in order to save the dead from the oblivion which the civic regulations of Florence as strenuously endeavour to promote. I never saw so almost universal a display of elaborate workmanship, and costly material, in any burying ground as in that of St. John at Nuremberg; nor did the honoured grave of Albert Dürer himself display more successful attention to its preservation than its bronze and marble neighbours.

But of all the sights of Nuremberg, I deem the matchless splendour of its painted glass to be the most remarkable; and to any one who has paid sufficient attention to this curious and now unknown art, to enable him to appreciate its almost inconceivable preëminence here, a circuit of a few scores of miles would be nobly repaid. There is much of this mysteriously beautiful work in various parts of the city, but it is in the fine old church of St. Lawrence that it is to be seen in the greatest perfection. The church itself is one of the great glories of Gothic architecture; but of these, Europe, (thanks to kind Heaven that inspired their builders) contains so many, that St. Lawrence might be merged and almost forgotten in the crowd, were it not for its windows, which are, beyond all comparison, the finest in the world.

These gorgeous pictures, that seem executed in jewels, surround the glowing choir with an atmosphere of magic light, which must be seen before any adequate idea can be conceived of its effect.

Nothing that is quite unlike all other things can be described; for where is one to find one's parallels and one's similes? I know of none that can assist me in conveying any notion of the choir of St. Lawrence at Nuremberg, either as to its general effect, or as to the grace and loveliness that comes forth upon examination. The window known by the name of " the Volk-amer window" has a sort of poetical harmony in its tone, which may sound very like nonsense

when it is talked about, but which very few, I
think, could escape feeling with a reality that
would surprise them, did they stand before it.

There is something churlish, invidious, and
disagreeable, in comparing old things to new,
for the purpose of declaring that our fellow-
creatures of the present day are lamentably
inferior to those who have gone before them.
I do not like the doctrine which would teach
us that we are degenerating, and I really have
no faith in it. But to state as a matter of
fact that the art of painting on glass exists
now, as it did in the days when the Volkamer
window was executed at Nuremberg, is worse
still, for such an assertion could be neither
more nor less than a positive falsehood, whereas
the doctrine of degeneration can only be considered as a blunder.

The restoration of the old churches of Bavaria have been performed in a style so infinitely superior in taste and skill to any similar
reparations which have been completed elsewhere (with the exception, perhaps, of some
portions of York Minster), that it is impossible
not to feel the highest admiration for the taste

and liberality of the royal patron who has presided over them all, and the very skilful and careful reparation of old painted windows has not been the least valuable part of the work; but even while enjoying the delightful transition from ruin to order, which has resulted from it, the not perceiving the strangely great inferiority of the new work to the old would only show that neither was examined with the attention they deserve.

It was probably some chemical accident which taught this lost secret to our ancestors, and it is certainly not impossible that a similar accidental combination may occur again; but till it does, we must be contented to study the effect which mere colour may produce on the imagination from the glass-painters of the middle ages.

There are multitudes of other sights to be seen in this grand old town, but they are, most of them, too systematically and too well pointed out to make it useful to dwell upon them here; I will, therefore, only venture upon one general remark, because it is applicable to more *free towns* than Nuremberg. Any one who will give themselves the trouble—and it certainly *is* trouble—to visit the dungeons and torture-chambers beneath the Rathhaus, will be made acquainted with one branch of the civic polity by which the power, prosperity, and *freedom* of this celebrated mart were secured.

The secret apparatus by which the discipline then thought necessary for teaching men what was good for them was administered at Nuremberg, reminds one of the many similar preparations having the same object, which are to be found in Venice, whose " thirteen hundred years of freedom" Lord Byron mentions with such deep admiration, while he seems so pathetically to lament that they are " *done*."

The day we visited this historic Rathhaus, the citizens were preparing the great hall as a dining apartment for the Germanic scientific congress, which was to meet at Nuremberg on the morrow; and I could not help thinking, although Nuremberg is no longer a " free town," that if the beatified spirit of the good Albert Dürer was permitted to recreate itself, by flitting about that splendid relic of its earthly inspirations, the triumphal car of Maximilian, so that he might listen to what passed below, it would be obliged to confess that, however much the fine arts and the fine commerce of the free town had withered away since it was painted, there was another species of commerce—namely, that of thought—which had prospered marvellously since its departure from the scene.

From Nuremberg we had an easy day's journey to Ratisbon; and though I and my companion had explored this city with a good deal of care before, we still found a multitude of objects which captivated our attention as effectually as when we had seen them for the first time. Among these was the noble and greatly improved cathedral, which, like the beautiful churches of Nuremberg, has been restored with so much good taste and so much antiquarian learning, that it may serve as a model to all church restorers for ever.

But the sight of sights, and the particular object for whose sake I am now endeavouring to prove that all comers and goers to and from Italy may find the taking rather a circuitous

urse a profitable mode of travelling, is the
ALHALLA. In the year 1837, we had seen
his majestic structure in progress, and had
hen conceived a sufficiently adequate idea of
hat it might be, to have made us very fre-
uently wish to look at it in its completed
tate, and, in September, 1845, we achieved
his object. Stupendously grand as are both
he site and the building itself, the approach
s disappointing, on account of the unfortunate
reponderance of the substructure, and espe-
ially of the upper terrace, which prevents the
uilding itself from being visible from the
ottom of the almost awfully bold flight of
teps which lead to it from the level of the
Danube. Could this substructure be made to
eceive any tint, save that of the white and
eautiful material of which the temple itself is
onstructed, the defect would be greatly reme-
lied; for then, at the point from which the
vhole structure becomes visible, the exquisitely
graceful form, and beautiful proportions of this
glorious edifice, would at once strike the eye,
nd create the unmixed and unmitigated con-
ciousness of exceeding beauty, which it ought

to inspire; but as it is, the temple, if I may use a hackneyed quotation, is the least part of itself, and the effect of its beauty at the first glance is very greatly lessened.

But this sensation of disappointment is speedily forgotten, when the platform on which it stands is reached, for, at that moment, I doubt if any imagination could exceed the reality of stateliness, grace, and splendour which meets the eye. I know no point of river scenery more superb than that which the Danube displays here, nor can I remember anything equal to the widely majestic extent of its smooth and silvery current, as viewed from the platform which surrounds the Valhalla, either on the Hudson, Mississipi, Ohio, Po, Rhone, Rhine, or even in the regal glory of the partially admired Thames at Windsor. There may be, and there are, many spots on the rivers I have mentioned (as well as on various minor streams), where rocks and forests give a wild, a picturesque species of beauty, of which there is no trace here; but as a scene of surpassing grandeur, both from its outline and its vastness, as well as from the indescribable air of majesty lent to it by this beautiful building, I know nothing that can come in competition with it.

All the world knows that the object of King Lewis of Bavaria, in causing this temple to be reared on the banks of the Danube, was to give as immortal a gathering-place as the earth could furnish for all the great celebrities of wide-spread Germany.

Both the idea, and the manner in which it has been executed, are perfectly accordant with all that we hear of this royal poet and enthusiastic patron of art, in every part of the country which he thus seeks to honour. A few such monarchs would add greatly to the value of railroads, by making the lands they rule over worth flying from one end of Europe to the other, to see; for such sights as the Valhalla must be seen by all who do not intend to die, and be buried, without having any idea how beautiful a marble hall may be.

Nevertheless, I would fain, if I could, give some little idea to the poor dear babes and sucklings, who are bound for a certain space to stay at home, some faint notion of this splendid specimen of German grandeur—not to mention the especial effort to which I have pledged myself, of endeavouring to convince the regularly migrating portion of my countrymen, that the most direct path is not always the best.

The approach to the Valhalla from Ratisbon is by a drive of two or three miles, the only interesting part of it being that which passes under the picturesque ruins of Donaustauf Castle. This castle and the little town at its feet form part of the principality of the Prince of Thurn and Taxis, who has a pleasant-looking summer residence at one extremity of the town. When last we visited this spot its general appearance was singularly wild and remote, and almost looked as if the siege which its castle withstood so nobly long, during the thirty years' war, were just over, and that the inhabitants had not yet settled themselves again comfortably in their rustic habitations. The growing wonder that was rearing itself within a quarter of a mile of its little territorial barrier had not, in 1837, greatly affected the air of profound repose which rested upon this ruined castle and its vassal tower, but now the case is different. The Valhalla has become one of the wonders of the world, and accordingly there are one or two gay-looking hotels which greatly alter the aspect of the place, for they seem to stand smiling upon all goers and comers to and from the imperial shrine, in the hope of tempting them to enter, either to prepare or repair the energies which have been called forth, or are about to be so, by the pilgrimage.

From this little town of Donaustauf there are two ways of approaching the Valhalla: the one is by remaining in your carriage, and mounting the steep road which leads to the table land behind the building; the other is by quitting it and proceeding on foot to the bottom of the colossal stairs, which, rising pretty nearly from the level of the Danube, conduct the bold climber to the portico of the temple. This latter approach is fatiguing, but incomparably the finest. The very labour of mounting the two hundred and fifty-five wide-spreading marble steps has a powerful effect, not alone upon the limbs *(bien entendu)*, but upon the imagination; and the very circumstance which is a defect, when observed from a

distance—namely, the disproportionate extent
of the vast substructure—becomes, as we cling
like pigmies to its surface, an additional feature in the general feeling of sublimity which
the stupendous edifice inspires.

I never remember to have experienced anything which much resembled the sensation produced by pausing at intervals in your upward
course, and looking down, deeper and deeper still
on the broad stream and its banks.   The brilliant whiteness of the vast marble surface over
which you are making your way renders a
frequent halt as great a relief to the eyes, as
to the limbs, and you turn round with glad-
ness, again and again, to look out upon the
wide-spreading landscape, despite the sensation of giddiness which the sheer descent, unmitigated by any species of balustrade, is likely
to produce.

Of course, the higher you go, the less likely
are you to see—throw back your head as much
as you will—any glimpse of the object you are
come to visit.   As you climb on, and on, and
on, nothing is to be seen before you but the
white expanse of huge Cyclopean masonry,

which seems, as it thus rears and spreads itself close upon the eye, to be extensive enough to encase a mountain. In this, I will not pretend to assert that I found beauty; but it produces a strange, and almost mysterious sense of vastness, which acts like a trumpet-note upon the imagination, and awakens and rouses it into a state exceedingly well suited to the business in hand.

When the highest terrace was reached at last, and we suddenly found ourselves standing before the double-columned portico of the majestic Doric temple, reared by a king in memory of the intellectual greatness of the vast nation of which his own kingdom makes part, I believe we both felt pretty strongly that we had not climbed for nothing. For myself, I fairly confess that something very like awe mingled with my admiration. The building itself, in its grand and severe simplicity, its pure and brilliant whiteness, and all the graceful majesty of its fine proportions, produced a thrill which it is not very easy to describe, but which it is very delightful both to feel, and to remember, and not the less so because there are so few occasions on which it is possible to feel it. We paused for a minute or two under this beautiful portico, and looked out upon the scene it dominates. The edifice, and the spot chosen for it, are marvellously well suited to each other. And then we turned to enter the majestic doors which a silent official stood ready to open for us. The whole scene, and every part of it, is wonderfully well calculated to turn the heads of all who are subject to visitations from that "*folle de la maison*," which, in sober English, we call Fancy, and could I at that moment have found leisure to propound the usually difficult inquiry—

> " Tell me where is Fancy bred,
> Or in the heart or in the head,
> How begot, how nourished ?"

I think I could have answered, without difficulty, " At Valhalla; a royal head being the father, a royal heart the mother, and poetry the nurse."

As the lofty door noiselessly gave way before the hand that touched it, I almost felt as if I were going to stand in the presence of the departed spirits in whose honour this antidote to a tomb was erected; and in good truth I believe that I trembled.

It will not do when one wishes to give an idea of any other earthly edifice, to prate about St. Peter's; but, in the way of confession, I may avow that the first words which passed between my companion and myself after we entered, were mine, and that I exclaimed, " Except at Rome, I have never stood in any building equal to this." And as I said it, I certainly had that greatest of earthborn miracles in my head.

Nevertheless, I do not mean to say that the temple of the Valhalla can soberly and rationally be brought into comparison with the church of St. Peter's. But there is in both some quality which seizes upon the soul, and rapts it in a sort of dreamy and vague elysium, before the judgment can find time to set about her graver work. I know that there are many other edifices besides the great *unique*, which I have mentioned, that might be justly quoted as superior in architectural value to the Valhalla. We may look at home, for instance, and find many such. The Minster of York could not be brought into competition with it gravely, without raising a smile. It stands, perhaps, in about the same relation to it as the Divina Commedia of Dante, to the Gerusalemme Liberata of Tasso. Yet, nevertheless, there is an unbroken completeness of beauty *in its own style*, which seems to set criticism at defiance, and which pampers the eye into such a state of measureless content, that it would require a strong and a painful effort to shake off the charm, in order to set about a learned inquiry concerning the comparative merits of something else.

On the whole, perhaps, it is good to have an eye with an appetite as universal as that of the bee, and with the same power of finding sweetness wherever it fixes. But if life were long enough to allow both of enjoyment and criticism, I should like to look twice at all that was best worth seeing, for the sake, in the first instance, of enjoying the agreeable impressions which a gratified eye brings home to one; and then to look at them all again, accompanied by some learned critic who should explain why it is that some objects, or combination of objects, so greatly exceed some others (of the same class) in their power of producing pleasure. For instance, as a case in point, why is it that the exterior of the Madelaine church at Paris produces an impression of more perfect beauty than the exterior of the Valhalla? And why is the interior of the Valhalla so incomparably superior to the interior of the Madelaine? I can easily imagine that persons of severe taste might think this interior of the Valhalla too gorgeous; but I cannot imagine that any could, on any ground, give the preference to the Madelaine. Neither of them affect to be simple, or severe, and the one which produces most powerfully the effect of graceful splendour, certainly succeeds the best; because the object aimed at is most effectually obtained. But why it is that the Madelaine fails so lamentably in producing this effect, I know not. Perhaps the strongest impression felt on first entering the Valhalla is produced by its peculiar and universal richness of colour, for its proportions are so perfect that its majestic size seems to escape observation.

The length of the interior is a hundred and sixty-eight feet, its breadth forty-eight, and its height fifty-three. This is a vast room; but it is its brilliance, and not its vastness, which makes the first impression. The walls are covered with the richly tinted marbles of the Untersberg, Bayreuth, and Adnet, which, as a background to the white marble of the busts, produces a beautiful effect. The floor also is of beautiful and highly polished marbles in Mosaic.

And having got thus far, I hardly know how to proceed, for I feel quite sure that if I attempt to enumerate all the varieties of colours and metals which contribute to the effect of which I have confessed my admiration, I shall not escape without some pretty strong animadversions on my taste. Nay, I am bound to confess, that upon reading a detailed description of the building before I entered it, I exclaimed rather vehemently against its gaudy colouring. I must, therefore, content myself with referring my critics to the same test which converted me. Let them go and look, and then find fault if they can.

And having said thus much, I shall proceed boldly, without mincing the matter, and care for nobody.

The ceiling, then, is of polished and gilded plates of bronze, dividing compartments painted light blue, and studded with golden stars. The roof, as well as the beams and rafters, are all of metal; the first of copper, the last of iron; and the light and graceful style in which this vast extent is sustained, is admirable. The transverse rafters, required of necessity for its support, descend from the ceiling in the form of three majestic pediments, which, instead of being a desight, are eminently beautiful, and converted into appropriate and very eloquent adjuncts to the whole design. They are filled by graceful and highly imaginative groups, in deep relief, representing the deities and heroes of the heathen mythology. The figures are of metal, partly gilt and partly coloured, but not gaudily—something between white and flesh-colour—and have at once a delicate and rich effect that is very pleasing.

At the height of about two-thirds of the entire walls a frieze runs round the whole building, and the length on each side is divided into three equal compartments. Below the frieze, these compartments are formed by masses of pilasters arranged against the wall; and above it are two caryatides in each compartment, which support the beams. These figures have been very accurately described in print already; but this description, notwithstanding its accuracy, produced such an effect in its detail, that if my companion and myself could have been scared from our Valhalla pilgrimage by the fear of seeing what was hideous, instead of what was beautiful, we should have turned our steps away from it the moment we had completed the perusal. The description mentions particularly their " ivory-coloured skin, their light brown hair, their gilded bear-skins, and their purple and white garments;" and the idea of beholding fourteen colossal ladies thus gaily dight, performing the office of caryatides in a temple dedicated to a purpose so solemn, had something really revolting in it. Even now that I recal these wild, but imposing monstrosities, and remember how perfectly well contented I was to see them there, I feel in doubt whether this is to be referred to the fact that Leo de Klenze, the celebrated Bavarian architect, who is said to have arranged the whole, understands the *trickery* of colour so well, that he may safely venture to defy all ordinary principles of taste in the use of it, or to my having been so bewitched by the spectacle altogether, as to have neither eyes nor judgment at leisure to criticise its details.

Whatever might be the cause of such indulgence, I gave the massive maidens absolution for all the gaudiness of their attire, and acknowledged the fitness of their presence as a deputation of warlike Walkyrian virgins, whose office it is to introduce warriors to Valhalla. Below the frieze, the compartments between the pilasters are covered by the splendid-looking red marble of Adnet, and in the centre of each is a female statue of white marble by the well known Berlin artist, Rauch. The middle one on each side of the room is standing; the one on each side of her, sitting. They are all winged, and represent some northern celestials, I believe—names unknown. In front of each group of pilasters is a very elegant white marble candelabrum; and between these, a massive Roman-looking arm-chair, of the same material.

Fronting the entrance are six Ionic columns of red marble, with white capitals; and above these is a balcony, from each side of which issues a sort of gallery, which runs along the two sides of the building over the frieze. But, standing below, you are not conscious of the existence of this gallery, nor is the balcony supported by the columns at the bottom of the room any desight; but, on the contrary, by lessening the effect of the great length, it improves the proportions of the hall.

The frieze, which is divided into eight compartments, three on each side, and one at either end, contains a series of mythological compositions by Wagner, who is said to have been engaged for ten years upon the work. They are modelled in deep relief in the beautiful white marble of Carrara, and are greatly admired, I believe, for the poetic richness of the composition; but to enter upon any detailed description of them would be an attempt equally bold and abortive. As ornaments of the noble hall in which they are placed, they fulfil their purpose well.

So much for this immortal hall—for immortal it must be to the fullest extent that earthly immortality can endure. Its marble walls, indeed, may crumble; but the memory of its erection, and of the noble thought which led to it, can never be forgotten as long as there are men left to remember what has been done by the great ones who have gone before them.

I have hitherto been speaking of the effect produced by the sight of the King of Bavaria's Valhalla; and as far as the eye is concerned, it matters little whose features are traced in the ninety-six white marble busts which already inhabit it; nor whose names, remembered after their features have been for ages forgotten, are inscribed on the tablets above them. To transcribe a catalogue of ninety-six names, plus sixty-four, would be tedious work; and yet the affecting to give a description of this remarkable edifice, without giving some sort of idea of the goodly company in whose honour its splendid roof has been spread, would be worse still.

I believe the arch-royal work of deciding who shall, and who shall not, enter into this Teutonic Valhalla, has been undertaken and performed by King Lewis himself.

There are but few mortals, I fancy, who feel any real matter-of-fact envy of kings and queens. Most people seem aware that there must be something a little fatiguing in the weight of a crown, notwithstanding the exhilarating consciousness of its brightness, and there are but few spirits of energy sufficient to covet such laborious greatness; but of all the royal offices that ever were undertaken, that which King Lewis of Bavaria has performed, and is performing, is the one which I think would shake my nerves the most. The refusing a monument in Westminster Abbey has been found to be rather a heavy responsibility, and sufficient to raise a cloud around the very reverend refuser's head too dense to be dispersed by any ray of the renown which he has left behind him. But what is this compared to a selection and rejection for and against the immortality of ALL "*belonging to the stems that speak the German language,*" from Arminius the great conqueror of the invading Romans, to Goethe the poet of Weimar! This is an awful undertaking.

Of the manner in which it has been performed, I am by no means capable of forming an opinion. King Lewis has published a little volume containing short notices " of the lives and merits of the great men who have been thought worthy of a place in the Valhalla." I have perused this little volume with attention, and it is, I think, impossible to do so without feeling that the royal author has a high and noble appreciation of intellectual greatness, martial renown, and ecclesiastical preëminence. But, nevertheless, there are some few names in this hall of immortals which might have been excluded without any very obvious wrong, and that of Luther permitted to enter, with less danger to the royal founder's orthodoxy, than its omission entails upon his justice.

That emperors, kings, and sovereign princes

should predominate is very natural and quite proper. Of these there are sixty-one out of the total number, amounting to one hundred and sixty.

Of warriors, there are forty-one; men of letters, thirty-four; bishops and saints, nineteen. The architects of Cologne and Strasburg have each a place. Three astronomers, Kepler, Copernicus, and Herschel. Of painters, there are nine; of musicians, four; and it is curious to observe how much better known to us are the great men who expressed their thoughts in language understood by all, than many very important royalties who figure in the list. Gluck, Handel, Haydn, and Mozart; Dürer, Vandyke, Von Eyck, Hemling, Holbein, Mengs, Rubens, and Snyders—we seem to welcome these with the interest of personal friendship, while the political and warlike great ones are greeted but coldly in comparison. Another thought that can hardly fail to strike one is, that the *right* which every head we look at has to its place, is in pretty exact proportion to the smallness of the addition which such honour can add to its glory. Whereas, there certainly are "some German gentles" there, who, but for their place within that gorgeous hall, might run some risk of being forgotten altogether.

THE VALUE OF A WORD.

THE VALUE OF A WORD.

———

THE following narrative is founded upon facts, and is, I believe, a tolerably faithful record of circumstances which occurred not very long ago in one of the central provinces of France.

* * * * * *

In a small provincial town, which, for the sake of avoiding asterisks, I will call Hauteville, there dwelt, a few years since, a very worthy old lady known by the name of Madame Perron. She possessed a very snug little income, and spent it chiefly in making herself as comfortable as she could. Perhaps, as she had not a relation in the world, she might think herself fully justified in doing so, particularly as she never spoke a cross word to any body, and did, now and then, bestow a few francs upon the poor. Her establishment was but small, consisting of one female servant, but that one was a host in herself, as she was willing to do anything, and was really capable of doing everything well. If it could, under any circumstances, be consistent with propriety, to assert that a maid-of-all-work was a person of genius—although she never in her life did, or attempted to do, anything that was not connected with her said business of maid-of-all-work—I might confess the having myself a strong conviction that Annette Bonvil was a woman of genius. Everything she attempted to do, she did well, and why may we not suppose that if she had attempted other things, things that had nothing whatever to do with the business of a maid-of-all-work, the same result would have followed? This idea had never suggested itself to Madame Perron, nor was it very likely that it should; but she really was as much attached to Annette as if it had. She considered her the best, and the cleverest girl she had ever seen in her life, and she valued her accordingly.

This excellent creature had lived with her old mistress for five years, having come quite as a girl in the first instance, to assist a grumpy old woman, whom good Mrs. Perron had not the heart to discharge, although she was quite past the age of useful activity; and certainly the hardest task that Annette, with all her genius, ever attempted to perform, was the keeping this old woman in tolerably good humour. However, she died at last; when Annette felt herself to be fully rewarded for all her forbearance, by being installed, not only chief, but sole attendant upon the venerable Mrs. Perron. Nothing can speak more plainly for the active industry of this young woman than the feeling that such a situation was desirable, for old Mrs. Perron was one of the most neat and particular old ladies in the world. But nothing seemed too much for the notability of Annette, provided she was permitted to perform her tasks in peace. So, after the death of the cross old housekeeper, everything seemed to go on well.

But Annette was not only very good, she was very pretty also; and like most other pretty girls, she had lovers. One of these was a young carpenter, who was as honest, active, and every way estimable as herself, and most truly did they love each other. Soon after Annette's emancipation from the old housekeeper, Louis Morel was emancipated from his apprenticeship, and it had been agreed between them, that if his business went on well for two years, they should marry at the beginning of the third. And nothing could be a more decisive proof also of the good character of Annette, and of the high estimation in which she was held, than the fact that her lover had obtained the consent of his parents—ay, and of his particularly well-married sister also, to his marriage with her; for the whole commune could not show a more thoroughly respectable couple than the Morels; their small farm was considered as a perfect model, and their small hoard of fairly-earned profits was increasing yearly.

As to the sister, she had made as good a marriage as it was possible for her to do, without falling into the misfortune of making a match that might have been called a *mésalliance;* for her husband, M. Verront, was the heir and successor of a well-established *epicier*, at Hauteville, and was an honest and honourable man, into the bargain; so that Louis Morel was rather proud of his family and connexions, and not without good reason. But they were all ready to receive Annette among them, notwithstanding her being a servant; and this circumstance being over-looked, there was indeed nothing at all imprudent in the match, for Mrs. Perron had made it well known to her lawyer that it was her intention to reward the faithful service of Annette, by leaving her a very comfortable little legacy. Under these favourable auspices, the life of Annette, though active and almost laborious, was a very happy one. Her gay spirits made everything she had to do a positive pleasure to her, and, better still, her gay spirits were the delight of her kind old mistress, who enjoyed her merry sallies and laughter-loving ways, as well as if there had been considerably more equality between them, both in age and condition.

But in every situation there is, as we all know, a peacock on the wall. The peacock that tormented Annette Bonvil, came in the shape of a lover called Nicole Starkie, a young journeyman butcher, as little like Louis Morel as possible.

One lover at a time is generally considered enough by most ladies; but if Annette had been as ugly as she was pretty, and the first word of love ever addressed to her had been spoken by Nicole Starkie, he would never have appeared to her in any light more agreeable than that of a peacock on the wall. In the first place, he was a coarse, vulgar, ill-looking fellow; and what was worse, he was one of the most worthless, ill-conditioned young men in the town. But, as a lover, he was at least constant; for above two years had passed since Annette refused his first proposal of marriage, and yet, not even the well-known fact of her being engaged to another prevented the constant repetition of his declaration that he could never love any one but her, and that if he did not get her, he must die.

As it was impossible, while living in the

same town, to avoid him entirely, poor Annette was very frequently exposed to the repetition of this species of persecution, till at length, wearied by the pertinacity with which it was repeated, her patience gave way, and she said, "Nicole Starkie, it is time that I should tell you, in case you do not know it already, that instead of loving you, I love another, to whom I am betrothed, and to whom I will be married, if married I ever am to mortal man."

The engagement of Annette was much too generally known at Hauteville for it to be possible for Nicole Starkie to be ignorant of it; but, nevertheless, when he heard her thus declare it to his face, his rage for the moment completely overpowered him, and clenching his fist so near her pretty face, as to make her draw back with closed eyes, he swore deeply and dreadfully that he would be revenged.

* * * * * *

The first of the two long years had nearly worn itself away, and Louis Morel was beginning to indulge himself with the occasional purchase of a few domestic articles, in order to

enjoy as soon as possible the exquisite delight
of feeling that he was preparing for his marriage, when an event occurred which converted
all his happiness to misery, and all his mirth
to mourning.

*   *   *   *   *   *

Upon a dark and dreary night, in the month
of January, old Madame Perron told her young
factotum that she felt inclined to go to bed a
full half hour earlier than usual, declaring
that it was too cold to sit up.

" Then you shall have your supper in bed!"
cried Annette, gaily, " and your supper shall
be your own darling *soupe au lait*, with collops
of thin bread, and *une bonne cuillerée de
rhum;* and if you do not sleep after that, I
shall wonder."

The old lady agreed to the prescription,
which was immediately prepared, and being
seated upright in her bed, very comfortably supported by pillows, and with a tea-tray steadily
arranged before her, with a sort of peculiar
skill, upon which Annette greatly prided herself, and to which her good mistress had
recourse whenever she meant to make her-

self particularly comfortable, the chartered favourite began to amuse herself and her mistress,
as she had often, under similar circumstances,
done before, by talking of her future prospects,
and of all the great things which she meant
to do when she should have become Madame
Louis Morel.

"Ay, ay," said the good-humoured old lady;
"I see how it will be. When you are
Madame Louis Morel, you intend to turn
into a perfect fine lady; but it is not so easy
a matter as you think for, Mademoiselle Annette. You are a good-looking girl enough; I
do not deny that; but you are not half so
delicate-looking as a fine lady ought to be, I
promise you. I do not believe, for instance,
that my shoes would be large enough for you,
even now, that I get them made half as big
again as they used to be."

"I don't know what to say about my feet,"
replied Annette, gaily; "but look you, dear
mistress! here is a leg for a stocking!" And
as she said so, she began making sundry cara-
coles, which certainly showed off the vaunted
limb to great advantage.

The old lady laughed heartily—so heartily, indeed, that she not only forgot her ailments, but so completely tired herself, that by the time her merry handmaid had removed the tea-tray, tucked up the bed-clothes, and drawn the bed-curtains, Madame Perron gave audible demonstrations of being fast asleep.

Well pleased to see her good mistress thus speedily released from her feeling of discomfort, and not much less so, perhaps, at finding herself mistress of a quiet hour that might fairly be called her own, Annette stole noiselessly from the room, leaving, as usual, a small night-lamp burning on the hearth-stone, and failing not to comply with the old lady's standing order of locking the chamber-door, and putting the key in her pocket. This locking her door was a measure of precaution upon which Madame Perron laid great stress. As long as nobody could get to her but Annette, she said, she knew she was safe; and, as a good loud bell was hung at the distance of about one foot from the pillow upon which the pretty head of Annette was nightly deposited, and the cord corresponding with it, at about the same distance from the hand of her mistress, there was a comfortable feeling of confidence on both sides that the communication between them was sufficiently prompt, and direct, to prevent any fear of inconvenience, either from the locking of the old lady's door, or the distance of Annette's apartment, although this distance was in fact about as great as the size of the little mansion would allow.

So the happy and innocent-hearted *fiancée* seated herself before her little work-table, and indulged herself till the authoritative tongue of the town clock proclaimed the hour of ten, in embroidering a few more sprigs on the square ends of a certain broad cravat which was destined to hang down over the breast of Louis M rel on his wedding-day. And most accordant to such an occupation were the thoughts of the pretty sempstress; for she thought of Louis Morel, and of him alone. His looks, his words, his noble conduct in loving her, poor and lowly as she was, in preference to all the gay lasses who were so constantly setting their caps at him, were dwelt upon with tender love. And then some particulars of a conversation which had passed between them on that very morning recurred to her, and she recollected with deep— oh, very deep delight!—that by having communicated to him an assurance, just before received from her kind mistress, of her being well remembered in her will, she had prevented his ever being reproached by his wealthy family for marrying a portionless wife.

But nevertheless, all this, delightful as it was, could not tempt her to betray the confidence placed in her discretion, by borrowing any more minutes from the night for the purpose of enjoying it, and therefore, no sooner had the town-clock, as above mentioned, struck ten, than Annette laid aside her dear precious work in its own pretty box, covered up a bit of burning wood in the ashes, to be ready for her mistress's early coffee in the morning, looked at the bolts and bars of her neat kitchen-door, and then crept quietly up stairs to her neat little bed-room. Prayer and thanksgiving were about equally blended in the nightly orisons of Annette, and rising from her knees, she dipped the rosy tips of her

pretty fingers in the little font of holy water
that hung beside her bed, and with a sweet
glance of mingled faith and hope beaming from
her innocent eyes as she raised them towards
heaven, she crossed herself, and laid down to
rest.

Though the life of Madame Perron's young
factotum was by no means one of hard labour,
there was sufficient activity in it to ensure
sound sleep to her, nor did she wait for it long,
for seldom did Annette lay her head for five
minutes upon her pillow, before she was fast
asleep. In less than half that time upon the
night in question, her eyes were already closed,
and the lulled senses had pretty nearly permitted their matter-of-fact labours to give place
before the vagaries of mimicking imagination,
when she was recalled to realities, by some
sound within the house, which she very
decidedly heard, but which, either from its
own nature, or from the distance from whence
it reached her, was so indistinct as to leave
her in doubt as to whether she had heard the
cry of some animal from without, or a human
voice more near, or, instead of either, the con-

cussion of some article that might have accidentally fallen to the ground in the kitchen, which was almost immediately under her. For a minute she lay with her heart beating in the painfully vague tremor which is sure to follow such sudden waking; but as all remained still, she speedily dropped to sleep again, while still asking herself the puzzling question, " What could it be?"

* * * * * *

Perhaps Annette did but sleep the sounder and the longer for having been thus awakened; at any rate, some of her neighbours, who were not only awake, but going to their work, while she was still dreaming of Louis Morel, were surprised to see the pretty well known balconied window of old Madame Perron, which looked upon the little orchard at the side of her house, wide open, while the door of the mansion was still closed, and no bustling Annette visible before it, in the act of making her portion of the pavement look cleaner than that which fell to the charge of any one else.

The first who passed was Dick Withers, the

son, who, though he knew the state of
nette's affairs too correctly to break his
rt by becoming her lover, admired her
ght young face too much to miss any oppor-
ity of looking at it, and as he saw the
n window, which fronted him as he walked
 the street, he paused for a moment before
 door, to give and receive the gay 'good
rrow,' which was often exchanged between
m. But the door opened not, and he
lked on.

Then came a blacksmith, and he too gave
look, both at the open window and closed
or, and then passed on.

But the next passenger was a washerwoman,
d one, too, frequently employed at the house,
d she made a decided halt. Washerwomen
vays know everything about everybody,
t in order to obtain this superior degree of
formation, they are of course obliged to seize
on every opportunity of acquiring it, and
erefore la Mère Durard could not think of
ing on to the house where she was to do
r day's work, till she had ascertained why
was that Madame Perron's bed-room window

was open, while the house door remained shut. She, therefore, very unceremoniously seized the brass knocker, and gave two vigorous blows with it upon the door. Annette was by this time up and dressed, and answered the appeal of this early visitor with a promptitude that showed that she must have been ready to leave her room, if she had not already done so.

"Good morning, good mother," said she, as, her bars and bolts withdrawn, she stepped out, with the kind smile and laughing eye that cheered every one that looked at her. "What brings you here this morning? This is Madame Monot's day, is it not?"

"Yes, my child, to be sure it is," replied the woman; "but how was I to pass your door, and see it still shut up, while the window of Madame was wide open, without stopping to ask if anything was the matter?"

"Madame's window open!" cried Annette, taking a rapid step forward into the street from which this window was so distinctly visible. "And so it is, sure enough!" she added, in accents of surprise; and then, without staying for further parley, she ran into the house again, and began ascending the stairs. But la Mère Durard was at her heels, and, catching hold of her gown, said, "You must let me go with you, Annette! I could not go to my work, if you would give me the world, without knowing if anything was the matter with the good lady."

" The matter with her, silly woman! What should be the matter with her?" returned Annette, with a little of irritation in the tone of her voice, arising from displeasure at any one's hinting that her dear old lady should be ill without her knowing it."

" Nothing, may be—nothing at all, Annette, dear; but only, you know, it does look odd to see the window open, and you to know nothing about it—doesn't it, my child?" Annette made no reply, but hastened on, and they reached the door together.

Annette's first movement was to seize upon the handle of the lock, which she did with some little agitation, forgetting, in her haste, that the door was locked; and, before she had sufficiently recovered her presence of mind to

take the key from her pocket, her companion
exclaimed, " And the door locked too! —
Oh dear! Oh dear! There is something wrong,
Annette!" And so saying, she began thunder-
ing upon the door with her fist, and exclaiming
vehemently, " Madame! madame! Open the
door, then, Madame Perron!" To all which
clamour no answer whatever was returned
from within, and Annette endeavoured to stop
it, by saying, "It is no use, Mère Durard!
Be quiet, then, I tell you!" While with one
hand in her wide pocket, searching for the
key, she employed the other in endeavouring
to withdraw her noisy companion from the
door. " What is to be done, then?" cried the
woman, impatiently; " do you mean to leave
the door without having it opened at all? It
is locked, that's plain. It is locked either
on the inside or the out, and how are we to
get at the key, I should like to know?"

" Here it is!" said Annette, in a faltering
voice, for by this time she too began to feel
frightened at not hearing the voice of her
mistress from within.

" What! You have got it all this time?

What on earth can the girl be thinking of ? Give it to me, girl! You tremble so, you can't use it. I'll open the door quicker than you will, by half."

And so saying, the Mère Durard seized the key, adjusted it in the lock, turned it, threw open the door, and entered, followed by the now pale and greatly terrified Annette.

The room was but a small one, and two or three steps forward brought them both to the bottom of the bed, and then a shriek arose from one or both of them that made itself heard for more than half way down the street. And no wonder, for never did a more ghastly spectacle meet the eye than that which the bed presented. The curtains, which had been drawn on both sides of it on the preceding night, were now pushed back on the side next the window, which being without either shutters or curtains, and now wide open, let in a flood of bright morning light upon the bed, and disclosed a sight that might have appalled the stoutest heart alive. The sheets, the pillows, the counterpane, were all not only dyed, but soaked in blood, and in the midst of it lay the pale and sunken features of the murdered Madame Perron. It was evident that she had bled to death, and when the woman Durard seized the bloody coverings of the bed, which scarcely seemed to have been deranged at all as to their position, and threw them aside, the manner of the murder became evident, for the jugular vein had been cut with considerable adroitness, and a small, but very sharp clasp knife was lying under the bed-clothes, close beside the corpse. Could any doubt have existed as to this instrument's having been the implement used for the atrocious act, it would have been removed by the fact that its blade and handle were both absolutely covered with blood.

Whether the piercing shriek with which this appalling spectacle was greeted proceeded from both the females who were the first to behold it, or only from one, may be doubted. Certain it is, that if poor Annette had power to produce such a sound, it must have been at the instant she first beheld it, for the next saw her stretched on the floor beside the bed of her murdered benefactress, as motionless and insensible as herself.

The Mère Durard was much too eager to narrate the horrible fact she had discovered to the whole town of Hauteville, to have any leisure to bestow upon the fainting girl, who was, therefore, left precisely upon the spot where she had fallen, while the less overpowered washerwoman rushed down the stairs and out of the house, screaming, " Murder! murder! murder!" with all the force of her very powerful lungs. This is a cry which cannot easily be listened to with indifference anywhere, but in the quiet peaceable little town of Hauteville it produced a degree of emotion which was as general as it was violent. Not a few females received it with a scream that sounded like the softened echo of the cry with which its first discovery had been greeted, while others stood or sat exactly in the attitude in which the ghastly news found them, as if turned by it to stone.

The male part of the population, however, took the matter differently. They all, or very nearly all, felt themselves called upon, both collectively and individually, to examine into and avenge this most horrible outrage upon their fellow-citizen. The house of the unfortunate woman was filled, in an incredibly short space of time, by a crowd collected from every class and profession; but the cause which had brought them together had something too solemn in it, to permit any violent breach of decorum among the orderly population of this remote little town, and those among them who from position and education were most fitted to assume authority, were speedily permitted to exercise it sufficiently to prevent any unseemly pressing of the crowd into the chamber of death; and this object being achieved, the prévôt of Hauteville, accompanied by his clerk, and attended by two medical practitioners, approached the gory bed, and an accurate statement was committed to paper, of the condition in which the corpse was found, as well as of every object around it.

When they first entered the room, the still senseless Annette was found lying on the spot where she had fallen.   The attention of the medical gentlemen was for a few minutes devoted to her, and so successfully, that her senses were speedily restored, and she was laid upon her own bed, with a friendly neighbour seated beside it.

This duty having been attended to, the next thing done was to call forward la Mère Durard, who, from being the first person that had entered the chamber of the deceased after the discovery of the catastrophe, was a witness of considerable importance.   As the reader is already perfectly well acquainted with all that she had to tell, it is needless to repeat it here, but every word was carefully committed to paper; and little as the washerwoman knew about the matter, her statement, together with her verbose commentary upon all she had seen, all she had heard, and all she had guessed, became as important in its result, as it was actually insignificant in its value.

Besides the persons already named, there were about half-a-dozen of the principal inhabitants of the town present at this examination, and some one among them, probably with no other reason or motive than the wish to avoid being totally silent and overlooked, observed that it would be necessary to examine the servant of the deceased very accurately, and with as little delay as possible.

When a dozen human beings are assembled together for some matter of grave importance, the not having anything whatever to say on the subject is apt to create a certain feeling of awkwardness among them that is embarrassing, and when this happens, the very slightest and most unmeaning observation is hailed as something worth having, and it is sure to receive rather more attention than it is worth. No sooner had M. Ambrose Lemaitre made this allusion to Annette, which he did with the grave, not to say solemn countenance which befitted the subject under discussion, than all the persons present began to look at each other, each throwing as much intelligence into the looks thus exchanged as their respective physiognomies permitted; so that in the course of about a minute and a half after the words were uttered, a very numerous progeny of thoughts had been conceived, all having Annette Bonvil for their object.

Now this was all perfectly natural; and perhaps it was no less so, that in the total absence of every shadow of evidence as to who had perpetrated the dreadful act which they were met to investigate, the idea that this poor girl had at least possessed the opportunity of doing it, suggested itself. Whether natural or not, however, so it was. There were, indeed, several who, when the suspicion found words, rejected it indignantly; declaring that Annette Bonvil was as good a girl as ever lived, and devotedly attached to her mistress. But there were others whom the very warmth of this defence set upon their guard against paying too much attention to it; and more still who whispered to their friends, that in such a case as this it was absolutely necessary that no foregone conclusions should be attended to, but that evidence, both positive and circumstantial, should be examined without any reference whatever to any preconceived notions of the parties concerned. That this was quite right and proper, nobody could deny; never-theless a very monstrous effect followed from it; namely, that a dozen honourable men all made up their minds to believe it *possible* that Annette Bonvil might have murdered her mistress.

Before the conclave separated, the state of the house, and all the property in it, was care-fully examined; but the room in which the deed was perpetrated was the only one in which robbery appeared to have been com-mitted. There, a bureau had been broken open, and if it had contained anything of value, it had been removed; for nothing re-mained but a few papers, among which, how-ever, was the will of the deceased lady. Some drawers and a press remained open; but little or nothing could have been removed from them, as, though somewhat in disorder, they were mostly filled with female vestments or with household linen. This examination having been completed, and copious notes upon every point committed to paper by the clerk of the prévôt, the self-appointed committee of in-quiry separated, the magistrate having locked the door of the fatal room, and put the key in his pocket. In the course of the day, a more formal *post-mortem* examination of the body took place; the cause of the death was declared to be the wound inflicted on the throat of the defunct, by which the jugular vein was severed, and the instrument, the small clasp-knife, which had been found lying beside her. Finally, a verdict of wilful murder was recorded against some person or persons unknown.

Annette, meanwhile, though completely recovered from her fainting fit, remained in a most pitiable condition. She wept incessantly, refused all nourishment, and seemed utterly incapable of listening to anything approaching the nature of consolation. To all that was said to her, indeed, she uttered not a word of reply, dolorously shaking her head, in token that everything that was said was of no avail, and only tormented her. In this manner, she passed nearly the whole of the day; but her eager glance towards the door of the kitchen, in which she sat, whenever it was opened by any of the innumerable persons who dropped in to see how matters were going on, shewed plainly enough that she did expect some one, towards whom, perhaps, she might not have preserved so rigorous a silence. But the hoped-for visitor came not, though almost everybody else in the town did.

It scarcely need be said, that this hoped-for visitor was Louis Morel, and the reason for his absence was such as to exonerate him from all blame, though poor Annette knew it not. It was a little before six in the morning that the call of la Mère Durard at the house of Madame Perron had brought to light the horrible catastrophe which had befallen her; and at a little before five, that is, exactly one hour before, Louis Morel had mounted his stout horse, and trotted gaily out of the town, in order to attend a cattle fair, at the distance of three or four leagues from Hauteville.

It was seven o'clock in the evening, and *pitch dark*, as such a state of atmosphere is expressively called, when he returned. If he passed any one, therefore, on his way to his father's house, he neither saw them, nor was seen by them, and accordingly entered the family sitting-room, looking as gay as when he had left it on the preceding evening, for no syllable of the tragic news had as yet reached his ears.   Within five minutes of his arrival, however, he knew it all; and it will easily be believed, that the state of his poor Annette was the circumstance which, even beyond all the horrors of the dismal tale, made the deepest impression upon him.

" You will let me bring her here, dearest mother?" he exclaimed, seizing the hat he had just laid aside.

" I expected that you would propose it, my dear boy," replied his mother; " and I would have gone to look after her myself, but I was told that everybody who entered the house to-day would be sure to get into trouble, by being called up as witnesses; and, besides, I know that she has been so surrounded by all the first gentlemen in the town, that I did not think it would be well for me to thrust myself among them.   But you can go, dear Louis, and bring her here, if she is willing to come; not that I expect she will consent to leave the poor body, dear good girl, as long as it is above ground." Louis waited for nothing more, and had traversed the distance between his father's house and that of the unfortunate Madame Perron in as short a time as it was well possible to go over it. But with all his haste, poor fellow, he came too late; Annette was no longer there. It was a good and a kind feeling which made those whom he found in charge of the house, and of the dead body it contained, reluctant to answer his questions; for they all knew that Louis Morel was the lover of Annette, and the sad intelligence which his eager questions elicited, at last, was, that Annette Bonvil had been taken to prison on suspicion of having murdered her mistress.

It would be folly to attempt describing the agony which this news caused to the unfortunate young man; if it were possible to do it, the effort would be unnecessary, for everybody may easily guess what his feelings must have been. Instead, therefore, of uselessly dwelling upon his sorrow, I must endeavour, as briefly as possible, to describe the species of evidence which was permitted to overpower not only all truth, but all probability, and thereby to plunge as innocent a girl as ever lived, into the most dreadful situation perhaps that it is possible for a *guiltless* human being to stand in.

This evidence consisted solely of the testimony of la Mère Durard, and the answers which Annette herself gave to questions put to her. The washerwoman had probably no feeling of ill-will whatever towards Annette, when the examination began; but as it proceeded, she gradually perceived that a strong feeling of suspicion existed against her, and that every word she uttered tending to increase it, was listened to with a degree of attention far greater than any words of hers had ever been listened to before. It is probable, too, that she herself, as she went on, began to think that all the pregnant questions asked had a great deal of wisdom in them, and that before the examination ended, the Mère Durard was pretty fully convinced that Annette had done the deed.

The limits of this little narrative do not permit my giving this curious examination at

length, but it was of a nature to prove, like
many others, that circumstantial evidence is
dangerous ground from which to judge the
innocence or guilt of a fellow creature. Annette had appeared greatly agitated. She had
attempted to open the door of the room,
although she had the key of it in her pocket.
She had resolutely refused to answer every question addressed to her. The knife, by means
of which the deed was done, was one evidently
brought from the kitchen, and not conveyed
through the window, so obviously left open for
the purpose of leading suspicion to some one
without, for the handle, by no means of a very
common form, was the same as that of three
others which were found in the kitchen; but
the one selected for this dreadful purpose was
greatly superior in sharpness to the rest. The
hour at which the Mère Durard had found the
door of Madame Perron's house still closed,
was decidedly later than that at which it
usually was opened. And Annette Bonvil had
dropped down in a dead swoon the moment
she cast her eyes upon the bloody corpse.

The answers of Annette herself, however,

probably went farther still towards convicting her. She owned, that she knew a gash across the jugular vein caused death, and as she made this avowal, as it was called, she became so pale, that those around her thought she would again fall into a fit. She owned that she had brought the knife into the room, and when questioned as to its peculiar sharpness, confessed that she knew it to be sharper than the others, and that she selected it for the purpose of cutting the bread thin. She confessed also, after being closely questioned on the subject, that she was aware of her being entitled to a considerable sum of money upon the death of her late mistress. She owned, that she knew the place where Madame Perron kept her ready money, and also, that she had not gone to bed quite so early as usual. When asked how the blood which in many places stained her dress, came there, her pallid countenance assumed an almost ghastly expression of horror, as she falteringly declared, she did not know. There was, moreover, a deep scratch upon the back of one of her hands, occasioned by its having come violently in contact, when she fell, with one of the screws which fastened the bed together. This wound had bled considerably, but it was certainly not her own blood which had left the large dark patches so dismally visible upon her petticoats. The lower part of her dress had, in fact, been not only stained, but in one part almost drenched in blood, by her having fallen where a stream of it had trickled from the bed, as long as the current of the poor victim's life had continued to flow.

These answers were all given with an hesitation and reluctance which made terribly against poor Annette, who nevertheless had not the slightest idea of the object with which they were asked. But her very soul was so shaken by the horrible event, that the being made to speak at all was perfect agony to her. When at last, however, one of her persevering examiners inquired whether she did not expect to be married to Louis Morel as soon as she got possession of her legacy, there was something so torturing to her feelings in thus bringing together what was to her the extremity of joy and of woe, that for a moment her reason seemed to give way, and instead of answering she uttered a fearful shriek, and suddenly falling upon her knees on the floor, threw her arms over a chair and hid her face upon them, as if unable to bear the eyes of those around her. Those eyes, meanwhile, exchanged many intelligent glances together; and though there were many good and honest men present, it may be doubted whether any one among them felt himself at that moment completely free from all suspicion against the innocent and greatly-suffering Annette.

Few words were exchanged among them, and those few were in whispers. "She must go to prison," muttered the most determined spirit among them. "Yes, I am afraid so," replied one of the most gentle. "If she be innocent," said a third, "a legal investigation will be the best means of enabling her to prove it." "No doubt of it," added another, in a tone that showed he was endeavouring to comfort himself by the belief. "You need not trouble yourselves as to the difficulties of the case," said the prévôt, sagaciously nodding his head. "That girl will confess before she has been in prison three days. I have had some experience."

And so Annette was sent to prison. But she did not confess. On the contrary, instead of appearing overpowered by discovering that she was suspected of having murdered her mistress, the naturally firm and healthful tone of her mind seemed restored by it. It required a minute or two to convince her that anybody really suspected her, and that her arrest was anything more than a matter of form; but once aware of this, her manner became wonderfully composed, and nothing in the least degree resembling terror could be traced in the grave expression of her lovely face. This perfect self-possession, however, did not seem to be fully granted to her till after her first interview with Louis Morel. A little expression of restlessness might have been traced in her eye till she had seen him. But for this consolation she did not wait long. As early as it was possible for him to get admission to the prison on the following morning, he was there.

On entering the room where she was, his

flushed cheek and flashing eye might have been read differently by different observers; but he rushed towards the prisoner, who had risen to receive him, and seemed as if he would have taken her in his arms.

"One moment, Louis!" she said, placing her extended hand on his arm, and holding him at the distance of its full length from her. "One moment! Let me look at you for a moment."

She did look at him. Their clear young eyes met, and exchanged one glance.

"That is enough, Louis," said she, gently approaching him, and laying her head, with an air of unspeakable confidence, on his shoulder. "Fear not for me. I can bear anything now. The inconvenience cannot last very long, I suppose? Only beg your dear mother to send me some needlework. But do not let any of them come to see me; it could not fail to give pain to both parties, and I am sure I shall do better without it. It is impossible that it can last long."

Louis understood her, understood her perfectly. The one inquiring look, the satisfied contentment that followed it; the wish for employment, and the no-wish to see anybody during her confinement but himself, were all comprehended and acted upon without a single question asked.

Annette was right in her conjecture that the interval before her trial would not be long. To say that she was not deeply affected when she found herself placed at the bar under the accusation of murder, would be nonsense. She was affected—strongly, profoundly affected; but she was not agitated. Both outwardly and inwardly she preserved her composure unshaken. Not once, no, not for a single moment, did it occur to her as possible that she could be found guilty—guilty of murder— guilty of cutting the throat of Madame Perron. Had she been accused of some lighter and more possible crime, she might have been uneasy; but as it was, she really felt more anxious about escaping the apologies and the compliments, and the fuss and publicity of her exit from the court, than for anything that was likely to happen to her while she was in it.

The examination of La Mère Durard was long and very tedious.   Then followed that of the two individuals who had looked at Madame Perron's door in expectation of finding it open, and had found it shut; and who had taken care to let everybody in the town understand how very great had been their surprise and astonishment at so very extraordinary a circumstance.   All this was listened to by Annette, who was permitted to sit down, with the same unvarying composure which had marked her manner throughout.

But when the *pleading* began, when she heard these, to her, seemingly unimportant details, twisted and turned, and commented upon till they seemed converted into proof positive that it was she, and nobody else in the whole world who did, or could have committed the murder, she looked up and around her at the crowded court, and in the faces of the judge and of the advocates, as if she had just awakened from a deep sleep, and doubted if she were not still dreaming.   There was one in the court, and one only, who watched her, and again understood all that was passing in her heart without the aid of words. But for the rest, they only thought that she was beginning to look very frightened, and they thought, too, that it was very natural.

At length the pleading was over, and the business of the jury began. We all know that a French jury has a great deal more to do than an English one. The verdict of a French jury is not restricted to the declaring whether in their judgment certain facts have been proved, or not proved, but is permitted to wander a good deal at large into the nature of the facts themselves, and also into speculations concerning the varying degrees of guilt which should be attributed under varying circumstances to perpetrators of the same crime. The trial of Annette Bonvil appeared a particularly favourable opportunity for the exercise of this privilege. And perhaps there was no circumstance through the whole proceedings which caused so severe a pang to the heart of the poor prisoner as the hearing her love for Louis Morel pleaded as an excuse and palliation for the act of which she was accused; for very eloquent was the appeal which this kind

defender made to the feelings of his brother
jurors on the natural power of love in a young
girl's heart, and the difficulty of resisting *any*
means of coming into immediate possession of
a legacy which would ensure her immediate
union with her lover. This very nearly overpowered her. She rose from her chair, and
was only saved from the indecorum of making
a pretty vehement attack upon the friendly
juror who had so ably exerted himself in her
defence, by the feeling of faintness which
caused her to drop back upon it. It was more
than usually long before the decision of the
court was made known; and when at length
pronounced, it appeared to satisfy no one.

The friends of the innocent it certainly could
not satisfy, inasmuch as it was so worded as
very plainly to indicate that a strong suspicion
attached to the prisoner; nevertheless, as,
after long debating, it was declared that the
perpetration of the deed had not been fully
proved, she was set at liberty, with a solemn
injunction to open her whole heart as speedily
as possible to her confessor, and strictly to

perform whatever penance he might enjoin for the sins of her past life.

And with this injunction ringing in her ears, and the figures of many old friends and acquaintances turning away from her, swimming before her eyes, Annette Bonvil walked out of the court.

She could not complain that any injustice had been done her. She had been suspected, tried, and acquitted. The suspicion, perhaps, was involuntary, the trial fair, the acquittal just. And yet she was no more the same in the estimation of her fellow citizens, than if a thousand murders had been proved against her. They could but look coldly on her then, and so they did now. Save Louis Morel, all looked coldly on her. He, indeed, did not look coldly; no, he looked as tenderly at her as he had ever done in his life, but he looked too miserable for that life to endure much longer.

Neither did his father, nor his mother, nor his sister, nor his brother-in-law, say anything harsh or unkind to her. But, then, they said so little, that it would have been hardly possible to find offence in it. It is true also, that instead of going back to the melancholy house of her late mistress, she was taken by Louis to the home of his family, and, far from being rudely treated there, she was told by his kind-hearted mother that she was quite welcome to make it her home till such time as she could make it convenient to get another for herself.

Her legacy was never talked of in her presence, for they all felt that the subject must be a very painful one after the horrible surmises which had been uttered respecting it. But in due time it was paid; and the melancholy Annette found herself the possessor of about twenty pounds sterling a year, which in that country was a revenue to live upon, but with a heart too nearly broken for her to be conscious of the slightest pleasure from the acquisition. Nevertheless, she was eager to take advantage of the independence it gave her, in order to withdraw herself from what she too surely felt to be the constrained hospitality of the Morels, *père et mère.*

To refuse their son's entreaty to take her
in, during the extremity of her distress, had
seemed to them [both impossible; but every
subsequent day had added to the feeling of
embarrassment with which this hospitality
was bestowed.   Nor would it be just to blame
this feeling; on the contrary, the indifference
with which the ready-money fortune of Annette was regarded, although it was sufficient
to have set their son up in his business in a
very advantageous manner, ought to be considered as a high proof of their honourable
feelings.

The love of Louis for his pale and drooping
Annette was as devoted, and, if possible, more
tender than ever, and had he not shrunk before the idea of breaking his mother's heart
and bringing the grey hairs of his father
prematurely to the grave, by marrying one
from whom every eye turned away with cold-
ness and suspicion, he would not have waited
for the expiration of the stipulated term, but
have married her instantly.   As it was, however, he dared not, and he did not hint at it,

and the miserable girl, having followed the grave, and seemingly reluctantly-given advice of the elder Morel respecting the disposition of her little fortune, took her melancholy way from the house that she now felt could never be her home, and hid her innocent head in the most remote and melancholy-looking lodging she could find.

Let it not be supposed, however, that Louis Morel either doubted the innocence of his affianced wife, or contemplated doing her the cruel wrong of breaking his faith to her; but there were still eleven months to elapse before the expiration of the time they had agreed to wait, and therefore, both from delicacy to Annette, and duty to his parents, he avoided the subject, feeling that the alluding to their marriage at so distant a date could but ill atone to her for not pressing for its celebration immediately; while the naming it at all, would have appeared to his parents, in the present state of their feelings, as a stab to the honour of their unblemished name, which it would be almost parricide to commit. He trusted that these feelings might in some degree be softened before the time originally fixed for his marriage arrived; but be this as it might, his resolution was taken, and he determined, if the state of feelings and opinions concerning Annette continued unchanged at Hauteville, to marry her there at the time appointed, in the face of all his kinsfolk and acquaintance, and then to withdraw both himself and her from its neighbourhood for ever.

The manner of her departing from his father's house was melancholy enough, and Louis, who had ventured to announce aloud his intention of accompanying her to her new abode, determined that he would not leave her without solemnly alluding to their engagement, and making her unequivocally understand that he considered this engagement as binding as ever. It was on the threshold of the door which led to her future home that Louis threw aside the restraint which he had imposed upon himself, and made this declaration, which he trusted would bring her comfort; but her manner of receiving it was greatly different from what he had expected.

" My dear, dear Louis!" said she, permitting

;h her voice and her eyes, for the first time
ce her trial ended, to express all the fervent
iderness of her heart. " My dear, dear
uis! you are dearer, much dearer to me
in ever, and you deserve to be so, for you
ve never wronged me by a doubting thought.
iu need not profess this, my own true Louis,
· I know it already, and it is *therefore* that
ove you better than ever, and it is *therefore*
it I will never, never, be your wife. Such
ing my resolution, Louis—and you have
ist enough in me to know that I am sincere
such being my resolution, you must agree
th me, that we must meet no more. No!
! we must not talk about it," she added,
:reating as he stretched out his arms to stop
r—" it would kill us! Farewell!" And in
instant she was out of sight, and sheltered
the dismal little room which she hoped
iuld hide her till the wished-for moment
me when it might be exchanged for her
ave.
She was quite right when she said that
iuis had trust enough in her to know that
e was sincere. He did know it, and at the

moment when he lost sight of her, he felt a pang at his heart that made him turn as white as ashes, and tremble from head to foot, as he stood.

* * * * * * .

It would be more easy, than either useful or agreeable, to follow these two unfortunate young people through the dismal nights and days which followed these events. Louis continued to repair daily to the spot where he had taken a workshop and yard, for the purpose of carrying on his business. But he did nothing that deserved the 'name of work; and to say truth, he had nothing to do. People got tired of his indifferent manner of receiving their orders, and of his dilatory manner of executing them, and took their jobs elsewhere. Annette had also a short daily walk to take, for she had her little loaf, and small measure of milk to buy. These together constituted her only food, and having procured them, she rarely left her room again till nightfall, and then she would wander for hours together along the lanes, and through the fields and copses which surrounded the town.

One morning she was going, according to custom, along a retired back street, in order to reach the baker's shop, when she remembered that she had need of some thread, which she had always been accustomed to buy in a more frequented street. But it was still very early in the morning, and feeling pretty sure that she should not meet any one, she ventured to turn from the narrow alley into a wider street. Her way led her by the butcher's shop, in which her former lover, Nicole Starkie, was employed, and immediately after passing it, she had to cross a dirty gutter which traversed the street, and with her long-learned habits of neatness, she crossed it carefully, to prevent her petticoats from being soiled.

She had not observed, as she passed the shop, that her old tormentor, Nicole, was in it; but so it was, and seeing the once admired but now degraded girl go by, he sprang forward to look after her. He reached the door just as she was in the act of displaying her pretty but coarsely clothed leg, by holding up her dress to cross the gutter. The young man uttered a brutal laugh, and clapping his hands, as he might have done if driving an offending dog before him, he exclaimed—

" There is a leg for a stocking !"

Annette heard his laugh, and also heard his words distinctly. She started, and then, for half a second, paused; it was no longer, for the pause was imperceptible, and she immediately pursued her way, with a step neither more nor less quick than before.

Did Annette Bonvil buy her thread and go home? No. She walked deliberately to the house of the chief magistrate, obtained his ear in private for about a quarter of an hour, and, within ten minutes after she had left him, Nicole Starkie was arrested upon suspicion of having been concerned in the murder of the late Madame Perron.

The rest of my story is already guessed at, and may be shortly told. The last idle words so gaily spoken to her poor mistress a few minutes before she left her for ever, had often recurred to Annette with a feeling of shuddering repugnance at their levity, and were therefore too well remembered to be listened to with indifference. Annette shuddered as she heard

them; but the instant afterwards, or rather
at the very same, the whole truth flashed upon
her. Nicole Starkie was the murderer of her
mistress! He must have been concealed in
the room during the last merry scene of poor
Madame Perron's life, and thus have overheard
Annette's boasting mention of her pretty leg.

Had Annette possessed both the will and
power to have spoken in her own defence before
her judges, with the same energy and eloquence
of truth as she used while now narrating the
events of that evening to the magistrate,
it is probable that the result would have been
very different. The effect it produced upon
him now was that of perfect conviction; and
his conduct proved that, however much he
might have blundered before, he only needed
to know what was right in order to do it. The
real assassin having been safely lodged in
prison, an immediate examination was made
of all the receptacles of property in his possession; and everything that had been taken
from the bureau of Madame Perron, even to
the little hoard of twenty double Napoleons
which Annette (before they were found) said

that she knew were kept in one of the drawers, were discovered among his things. Among them also were several articles of plate, which several of the neighbours swore to having seen displayed at the old lady's little tea-parties. In short, there was proof amply sufficient to condemn him. And condemned he was, to labour in the galleys for life; capital punishment being very rarely resorted to in the country of which I am speaking.

Have I anything more to tell? Can anybody doubt that Annette Bonvil became the happiest of wives, and that the whole Morel family were proud enough of their connexion with her to have spoiled any girl in the world but herself?

CONRAD REINHARDT.

CONRAD REINHARDT.

"But your village has a bad name with the Emperor's custom-house officers, I am told," said I to my host's pretty chatterbox of a daughter, at a primitive little hostelry on the banks of the Inn. This said village was Martinsbrück, a secluded little place at the lower extremity of the lower Engadine. One of the rut-and-rock defying cars of the country had deposited us there the previous evening, weary with a long day's mountain travelling, and with admiring the wondrous scenery around — fatiguing occupations both. Our most eager requisitions had been for beds—the more so, as we were to be once more a-foot by

five o'clock the next morning; and despite the
activity on which I pique myself, I was not
very sorry when the five o'clock came, to see
from my little window, as I looked out through
it from beneath the wide eaves, towards the
Inn, that the rain was descending in such
torrents as fully to justify me in turning
round, and re-nestling myself on my pillow.
It was evident that we were there for the day,
and that we might consider ourselves as very
fortunate if it proved to be for one day
only.

Under these circumstances, an hour or two
lost in oblivion was a decided gain. But with all
the good will in the world to indulge in laziness,
the full activity of summer travelling was too
strong upon me to let me by any possible
device delay the commencement of the day
beyond eight o'clock. Neither could breakfast, despite the exquisite daintiness of mine
host's cream and honey, be prolonged much
beyond half an hour; and when that was over,
the rain still pelting piteously, I was well inclined to welcome the ready gossip of the
bright-looking, sweet-mannered girl who came

ostensibly to remove the breakfast-cloth, but in reality, I suspect, for the express purpose of enjoying a little chat with visitors from beyond the world of her native valley.

She really was as pretty a specimen of a Swiss maiden as ever milked cows on an upland pasture, or rewarded with a smile the victor of a village shooting-match. Educated, too, she was, for she could talk French as well as German, besides her own native *patois*, could read, write, and cipher, spin yarn, make butter and cheese, and work embroidery. In a word, Bertha Weber both was, and deserved to be, the queen of the village maidens of Martinsbrück. A most fierce and enthusiastic little republican, too, was she, and very plainly gave it to be understood that she deemed a free Protestant citizen of the Grisons to be a very greatly superior person to a Tyrolese subject of Austria, who paid taxes to the Emperor, and tithes to the priest at the other end of Martinsbrück bridge. It was, therefore, in reply to some self-gratulating depreciation of her neighbours, the subjects of his Imperial Majesty of Austria, that I used the words repeated above—" Your village has a bad name with the Emperor's custom-house."

" Why then," retorted the little republican free-trader, with a toss of her head, and a flash of her bright young eye—" why then do kings make laws which interfere with the honest trade of industrious folks who, by the favour of God, have nothing to do with kings or kaisers?" This was very like an admission of the accusation; and, in truth, it is well known that the inhabitants of Martinsbrück are inveterate smugglers.

Contraband trade, however innocent the traffic may be in itself, is not only illegal, but really immoral in its tendencies and results, by the very fact of rendering those engaged in it enemies to the law. If eating potatoes were declared by law infamous and criminal, those who eat them would infallibly become not only conventionally but really and truly immoral and degraded; and so it is, and so it must be with the smuggler, the poacher, and many another offered up by necessity as a social sacrifice to civilization.

But then, it must be remembered that the

good people of Martinsbrück are criminals only on one side of the river, and that side not their own. They are rebels only against a law which their country does not acknowledge. The public opinion of their own people is with them; and the bold smuggler, who is an out- cast and a vagabond on the Austrian side of the frontier, is a hero, as well as a very re- spectable member of society on the other. And for this reason I beg to observe that my friend, Bertha Weber, must be excused by the well- behaved and orderly denizens of Cockney-land, although she may have learned to regard con- trabandists and their trade with other eyes than those of a revenue officer. In truth, the topographical peculiarities of this part of the boundary line of Austria's vast frontier, render an effective performance of the Imperial dou- aniers' duties exceedingly arduous, and almost impossible.

Two good roads, that from Italy over the Stelvio, and that from the heart of the Tyrol, by Brixen and Meran, meet near the little town of Mals, in the upper valley of the Adige. That river, under its German name of Etsch,

is here in its infancy; and the road proceeding
up its valley in a northward direction, soon
reaches the low-shored, ugly, marshy lakes in
which it takes its rise, passes along the margin
of them, then crosses the Reschen, the lowest
of all the passes over the Alps, which here
sink to a very remarkable depression, and form
the *watershed*, as it is called, between the
waters of the Adige and those of the Inn, and
thence descends beside one of the tributary
streams of the latter till it reaches the great
valley of the upper Inn, and the river itself at
a spot a little beyond the town of Nanders.
Here the road enters the magnificent defile
celebrated as the Pass of Finstermünz, making
the already majestic river its pioneer through
the rocky barrier, and following its more tranquil course onward through the fertile province
of the Ober-Inn-thal. Thus the road joins the
Inn at the spot where the river issues from a
tremendous chasm that its waters have formed
for their outlet from the Swiss valley of the
Unter Engadin, and passes, though without
touching Switzerland, close along its frontier.
The Pass of Finstermünz is known to all the

world of travellers and picturesque-hunting tourists. The pass is undoubtedly a very strikingly beautiful pass, and it is celebrated because the high road runs through it. Many a man, and many a thing, besides Finstermünz, have enjoyed celebrity from analogous causes, and owed their reputation to the lucky chance of not being out of sight.

Few among the multitudes who annually linger (a little while) to gaze at the renowned beauty of this Finstermünz are at all aware that a far, far finer pass is within a few yards of them. Even the much smaller number who go from the Unter Engadin into the Tyrol are not aware of it. These follow the Inn till they arrive at Martinsbrück; they there cross the stream by the bridge from which the village is named, enter the territory of Austria at the foot of the bridge, through a custom-house toll-bar, in a very legal and proper manner, and then ascending the hill by a pretty zigzag road through the forest, fall into the before-mentioned highway at the town of Nanders, distant from Martinsbrück about four miles. So that a traveller of the legal and respectable sort going from Engadin to— say Landech, would leave the river Inn at Martinsbrück, reach the great road at Nanders, and again meet the river as it enters the Finstermünz pass; and this is the only road recognised by the Emperor and his officials, or known to sober-minded, steady-going travellers, and a very beautiful road it is, and quite bold and sublime enough for the nerves, as well as for the consciences of well-behaved, orderly, law-observing citizens.

But a portion of the river, it will be observed, has been lost sight of by the traveller following this route. The high road, and the law, go this way—the river, and the contrabandist, take another. The mountain, which the road from Martinsbrück to Nanders climbs by slow zigzags, is cleft by the more impetuous hurry of the river, and the result of this turbulence is a pass, compared to which the succeeding one of Finstermünz is as one to a thousand. I rather fear that my reader may think I have been unnecessarily tedious in my topographical explanations, but it was really necessary for the right understanding of the story I am going to tell him that he should, if possible, have a clear idea of the localities; but after all, perhaps, a glance at a good map might do more towards obtaining this than all which description can accomplish.

The passage which the Inn has thus made for itself from the Engadin to the Ober-Jun-thal, is in truth one of the most magnificent, not to say tremendous defiles conceivable. The river itself forms the boundary line between Switzerland and the Tyrol, for the distance of the two or three miles occupied by this gorge, and the path, such as it is, starting from Martinsbrück, leads along the Swiss, or left bank of the stream. This side is by far the least precipitous. The opposite cliff is called the Nicholaus Mauer—St. Nicolas wall, and a wall it may well be termed, but such a one as human architect never has constructed, and never will construct. At the foot of this mighty wall, dashes the raging river, deep and strong, yet angry and noisy as a brawling brook. The opposite, along which the smuggler's path finds its way, is steep, rough, and rocky enough, and there are some points at which the said path cannot be followed without a little difficulty; not that there is anything which an active walker, with a tolerably sure foot, need wish to avoid. The merely traversing this path, however—though the doing so in all weathers, in darkness, and with a heavy burthen upon the shoulders, is no child's play—the merely traversing this rugged path, is far from being all that at all times is required from the Engadin smugglers in order to bring their merchandise to its journey's end in safety.

The following tale, which was recounted to me by my pretty friend Bertha, during the long wet day I spent at Martinsbrück, will enable those who read it to form some idea of the sort of exploits which these men are not unfrequently called upon to perform, and may lead them to understand readily enough why it is that the successful smuggler is a hero in the eyes of the maidens of these vallies, and why he is likely to prove a successful lover, as long as female hearts are to be won by the same means that Othello took to win that of Desdemona.

Conrad Reinhardt, however, as the reader will see, had nothing to do with the heart of my little Bertha; a fact which I state at once, to prevent any misunderstanding as to the source of my pretty friend's emotion. But nevertheless, she told me his history with such a play of feature, and such alternate flashing and melting of her fine blue eyes, that I found it impossible to listen to her without sympathy. I will, in repeating it, follow her narrative as closely as I can; but her pretty manner of telling it, must be supplied by the imagination of the reader.

" The articles which form the objects of contraband trade between this part of Switzerland and the neighbouring territory of Austria, are manifold. Salt and tobacco are among the most important; but coffee, tea, and certain sorts of manufactured goods, are also introduced in considerable quantities, despite the vigilance of the imperial revenue officers. But there is one other article, whose introduction is yet more vigilantly guarded against than any of the above named commodities, and for which nothing save the daring hardihood of the smuggler can obtain admittance. I allude to prohibited books. It is probable that the importation of such wares, which are as yet by no means in very general request in Austria, would fail to remunerate the contraband trader sufficiently to induce him to undertake the risk and labour of establishing such a traffic, were not a less doubtful one already organized for the supply of more material wants; but a regular contraband trade being thus already in action, those engaged in it are often employed in the manner I have alluded to.

It was upon an enterprise of this latter sort that the Conrad Reinhardt I have already mentioned was employed one dark and stormy night, towards the end of February, some few years ago. Conrad was then quite a young man, not above two-and-twenty years old, or thereabout; but he was already a daring and experienced smuggler; for his father had been a smuggler before him, and he had been as regularly brought up to the profession of arms

against the Austrian dominions, as the sons
of noble races elsewhere are brought up to the
same profession on a somewhat larger and more
splendid scale.

Conrad Reinhardt, notwithstanding his particularly regular education, was certainly a
very young man to be entrusted with an important undertaking of the kind alluded to;
but he was thoroughly well known to his
employers, and had approved himself not only
a bold, intrepid, yet in fit season a very skil-
fully cautious smuggler, but moreover an
honest and perfectly trustworthy man.   And
in the valley of the Engadin this too is necessary to completing the character of a good and
esteemed smuggler.   Sometimes the professional contrabandists carry on a considerable
trade on their own account; much of the
goods which they thus surreptitiously convey
across the frontier being their own property.
But more frequently, and especially in ven-
tures of a valuable description, the smugglers
are only the kind carriers of quiet stay-at-
home merchants, who risk nothing but their
capital, while they absorb by far the largest

portion of the gains arising from the perilous and most laborious achievements of the poor smuggler. And thus the trustworthy integrity of the hired heroes employed in the traffic is quite as important a matter to their employers as their skill and intrepidity. Nor is it a trifling praise for the poor inhabitants of this law-defying valley of the Engadin, that rarely, if ever, has an instance occurred of one of these daring fellows betraying the trust reposed in him.

On the occasion in question, Reinhardt was to quit Martinsbrück about ten o'clock at night, with the dangerous pack of prohibited wares, which it was hoped he would be able to deliver safely at a certain house in the town of Flanders, at about two hours after midnight. A moonless night had of course been selected for the enterprise; and the circumstance of its turning out a very stormy one also, was deemed by the dauntless young smuggler and his friends as considerably more favourable than otherwise. Not, indeed, that the revenue officers, whose vigilance it was his business and his duty to elude, were at all less likely to be abroad upon that roaring, blustering night than upon any other. Both parties were too well accustomed to the habits of each other, and too much inured to doing their work at all seasons, and in all weather, to hope for any remission of peril on that account. But, nevertheless, the increased darkness, the increased roar of the river, and the general hurlyburly of the elements, added very materially to the facilities of passing untracked, unseen, and unheard.

It would be an odd spectacle for the peaceable inhabitants of a snug, well-sheltered town, to watch the eyes of love, of watchful maternal love, for instance, eyeing with satisfaction the black, starless sky, and smilingly listening to the roaring waters and the blustering wind, just as her darling hope, her noble-hearted boy, is about to take his heavy-laden midnight walk along the narrow, slippery path that skirts the raging river, whose thunders she can hear distinctly, though beneath the shelter of a distant roof! Yet so it is, and so it was upon the very night that young Reinhardt set off upon his eventful expedition across the frontier.

But before we actually start with the bold Conrad upon this hazardous enterprise, it is necessary to the right understanding of what is to follow, that the reader should be let into the secret of a little bit of the young contra-bandist's private history. It is about an affair of the heart, *cela va, sans mot dire.*—It is unquestionably a matter of course, and as love-making is in essentials very much the same thing whether a Swiss smuggler or an English gentleman be the performer, I shall not deem it necessary to enlarge upon this part of the matter. But it is necessary that I should make the reader acquainted with one or two particulars respecting the person who held Conrad's heart in her keeping.

This was a certain Ida Bradela.

On the flank of the mountain that forms the Swiss side of the gorge through which the river Inn rushes, and along which our young smuggler's path lay, there is, about half way between Martinsbrück and Finstermünz, a solitary cottage, perched amid rocks, forests, and waterfalls, but surrounded by a few roods of cultivated ground, snatched, as it were, from the savage chaos around, by hard, bold, and patient labour. This was the property of Ida Bradela's father, and this cottage was Ida's dwelling. It was a wild-looking, unpromising looking, little freehold enough, but it *was* a freehold, and the Bradela family lived there in content, and in good repute among their neighbours of the valley, though the little rocky farmlet kept its master poorer than the generality of the farmers of the dale. By Bertha Weber's account, this Ida Bradela was decidedly the prettiest girl in the Engadin. All the men were in love with her, and most of the lasses declared that they could not see the reason why——a sort of two-fold testimony this, which sets the pre-eminence of Ida's beauty beyond controversy. The matrons, indeed, except a few who had daughters with pretensions high enough to compete with those of the beauty, *par excellence*, were of the young men's faction, and had ever a good word and a kind welcome for Ida Bradela; for she was a good girl, industrious, modest, and doated on by her parents, to whom she was the very best of daughters. But though the

lone cottage of which this peerless girl was a
contented inmate, stood secluded, and apart
from all other dwellings, in the midst of its
little rocky domain, it was not at so remote a
distance as to preclude its inhabitants from
descending into the valley whenever either
business or amusement called them thither, and
" the beauty" of the Engadin was therefore
far from being unknown among the *grand
monde* of her neighbourhood. In truth, not
a fair, nor a shooting-match, would have been
deemed worth going to, had the beautiful Ida
refused to grace it with her presence; and
both happy and proud was the youth who
could succeed in securing her hand for the
dance which invariably concludes the village
merry-makings.

In addition to the natural propensity of the
female heart to favour those of the male sex
who voluntarily and undauntedly engage in
deeds of enterprise and danger, it must be
confessed that the youths engaged in the contraband trade of the Finstermünz enjoyed yet
another advantage in their rivalry for the fair
Ida's favour, over the more quiet and peaceful

swains of the valley—namely, the highly and justly prized one of *opportunity*. The Bradela farm was the only house in the track of the smuggler, between Martinsbrück and Finstermünz, and this threw in their way a very precious chance, which it will easily be supposed was not lost upon the young free-traders. Neither, indeed, did the seniors of the profession much less frequently avail themselves of the hospitable shelter of old Johann Bradela. They were all, in fact, well known at the farm, and various were the mutual good offices exchanged between its inhabitants and the hardy adventurers whose calling led them to pass within a few paces of its little gate.

Well, to make a long story short, Conrad Reinhardt, the hero of my tale, was at length admitted and recognised as the favoured lover and betrothed husband of Ida Bradela. His principal rival, not so from any wavering preference of Ida, but from the vehemence of his own passion, had been a young farmer of the valley, named Carl Levette. He was of French origin, his grandfather having settled on the farm which he himself held at the period of my story. Now, it so chanced that on the Friday preceding the Saturday which had been fixed for Conrad Reinhardt's expedition, the pretty Ida had been sent with some farm produce on a marketing expedition, to a place at about a mile's distance up the valley, and it also chanced by one of those remarkable coincidences which do sometimes occur in the histories of lovers, that my smuggling hero, having nothing better to do, had also strolled up the valley towards Strada, and had by accident fallen in with Ida, as she was returning homewards from her marketing trip.

Their path to Martinsbrück lay across Levette's farm, and as they passed near his house, the rejected suitor came out, and, unwelcome enough, as we may well guess, joined, and walked on with them. Reinhardt, however, flattered himself that he would accompany them only to the limit of his own fields, and thus managed to keep his temper in good order, and behaved with perfect civility. Thus they walked on together, till, at a gate which formed the boundary of Levette's property, the young farmer, apparently about to quit them, stopped, and said—

" Well, Conrad! you free-traders have an easy life of it! How much longer do you mean to take your ease at home here, living like a gentleman, and taking these pleasant afternoon walks with Miss Ida?"

" Not much longer, Carl—worse luck! I shall be off up the hill again to-morrow night," returned Reinhardt.

" So, then," said Levette, " you wont be at the rifle-match at Schnols, on Sunday? You will hardly get your cargo delivered, your accounts settled, and all the business done and finished, in time to get to Schnols for the meeting, put what good-will you may to it. So, with Miss Ida's permission," he added, turning to the beautiful girl who hung upon her lover's arm, " I shall once more have the honour of a dance with her, Conrad, before she changes her name, which will be sure to happen before long, I suppose. It will be my last chance; and I well know, my fine fellow, that I should have none at all, if you were to be there."

" And, faith," replied Conrad, laughing, " I

would not advise you to count on that with too much certainty. It will be sharp work, there is no denying that, Master Levette—very sharp work, to get my business done at Nanders, and be in time for the rifle-match at Schnols, on Sunday. But who knows what a willing heart and a light pair of heels may do, when the reward of making good speed is a dance with such a partner, and mayhap something else into the bargain," he added, with a sly look into Ida's laughing eyes, which gave the lie to the protest entered for form's sake by her blushing cheeks and pursed-up little mouth.

" Very fine talking," retorted Carl Levette, " but you will never be at Schnols next Sunday."

" We shall see," said Conrad.

" Will pretty Miss Ida promise to dance with me if you are not?" demanded Carl, turning to the blushing girl.

" Promise him, Ida!" said Conrad; " promise him! and trust to me," he added in rather a lower voice, " to save your promise, and provide you with a partner who will, I hope, be more agreeable to you."

Ida immediately gave Levette the required promise, and the trio separated; the young farmer to return to his house, and the lovers to pursue their delightful walk down the valley to Martinsbrück.

The above conversation, though it had passed with apparent good humour and friendliness on all sides, had not failed to wound Carl Levette to the quick. He had, by joining the acknowledged lovers, placed himself in a position which was equally sure of producing pain to himself and annoyance to them; and the sight of their mutual satisfaction and perfect happiness in each other, the sort of intimate intelligence between them, and their air of indifference as to whether he was pleased with it or not, had nettled him to the soul. Above all, the sort of defiance which Conrad's words to Ida about the promise implied, and the insolent triumph, as it seemed to him, of the little sotto-voce addition of the successful lover, of which not a word had escaped the sharpness of his jealous ears, sent him to his lonely home in a fearful paroxysm of mortification and jealousy.

An hour of silent, solitary meditation on this scene sufficed to suggest a project of revenge, and finally led him to determine, at all hazards, to prevent the speedy return which Conrad so confidently anticipated, and thus to secure to himself not only the performance of Ida's promise, but such a triumph over both the lovers, as might atone to himself for at least a part of all the misery he had endured.

Carl Levette had not the reputation in the valley of a wicked, or spiteful man. He would have been deemed by his neighbours to be utterly incapable of intentionally doing that which, nevertheless, he in fact brought about; and we must therefore hope that the utmost result to which he looked forward as the consequence of the measures he adopted, was the temporary delay of Conrad's return. But in any case, he did that which would have seriously endangered his life in the Engadin, had it become publicly known to the inhabitants of the valley. This deed was nothing less than furnishing information of the young smuggler's intended expedition to the Austrian authorities.

The remainder of that day, and the greater part of the ensuing night, were employed by him, as it afterwards appeared, in obtaining accurate information of the exact nature, time, and subject of Conrad's approaching enterprise. In accomplishing this, he was but too successful, and in the early morning of Saturday, before the earliest dawn of light, and long before any of the villagers were on foot, he crossed the bridge at Martinsbrück, at the Austrian end of which there is, as above stated, a post of custom-house officers. He was of course stopped at the foot of the bridge by the soldiers on duty, and being conducted to the officer commanding the post, stated to him the nature of his business. It might perhaps have appeared to the Austrian, that so unmotived a piece of treachery, might be only a hoax, or a stratagem to cover some ulterior smuggling project, rather than a *bonâ fide* intention to assist the Imperial revenue officers. But this obvious danger was very ably guarded against by the informer's declaration that having preserved the faith which his grandfather had brought with him to the valley, he could not with a safe conscience permit books which were hostile to the holy catholic faith to be introduced among a nation of true believers. He acknowledged that it was a matter of perfect indifference to him how much salt, and tobacco, found their way across the frontier, but not so as to the soul-destroying cargo of heresy which he had learnt was to be the object of the present expedition. This explanation sufficed for his purpose. Whether the officer deemed him most a scoundrel for his treachery, or a saint for his religious zeal, matters not; it is enough that he believed his story, sent him back safe across the bridge, and immediately set about taking the necessary measures for ensuring the capture of poor Conrad, and his dangerous packet of anti-papistical wares.

But while fate, in the person of a custom-house officer, was thus weaving in a dismally dark thread into the woof of my hero's destiny, his good genius was not altogether idle, but was actively employed in preparing some web of brighter tint that should make up the chequered tissue of which the life and lot of mortals is composed. And this she accom-

plished by the unconscious agency of old Johann
Bradela, the fair Ida's father; for it so
chanced that the good farmer had gone on
Saturday to Noberts, a little village between
Martinsbrück and Nanders, and consequently
in the Austrian territory, for the purpose of
investing some money very carefully scraped
together, in the purchase of a cow which was
for sale there. I learnt, from my dear little
Bertha Weber, the whole history of the causes
which led the envied owner of this excellent
cow to part with her, but as these particulars
are not essentially necessary to the develop-
ment of my story, I shall omit them.

It may be as well to record, however, that
Johann had intended to go to Noberts on the
Friday, but Ida had said to her father, " No,
father,—do not let us both go, and leave my
mother alone. I *must* go down with the butter
to-morrow, you know, but you may very well
put off your going till Saturday." And Johann,
like a truly wise and good man, acted in the
manner his daughter suggested. Whether
our dear Ida had any second motive besides
the one assigned, concerning the solitary con-

dition of her mother, we will not pause to inquire. Now there was one circumstance which, as Bertha said, really was exceedingly curious, and looked most wonderfully like the special interference of Providence. Johann Bradela might have gone to Noberts either by Martinsbrück or by Nanders; in the first case, he must, on leaving his own mountain homestead in the gorge of the river, have proceeded *up* the stream to Martinsbrück, have crossed it there, and so on to Noberts by the Nanders road, or, in the second, he must on leaving home have journeyed *down* the river as far as Finstermünz, crossed it by the bridge there, and so have proceeded by the high road to Nanders, and thence to Noberts. This latter is rather the longer way, but it so happened that it was, nevertheless, the one chosen by Johann Bradela upon the occasion in question.

He had left home after breakfast, and, having passed through Nanders, was turning out of the great high road into the bye-way across the hill which led to his destination, when he met four Austrian soldiers, and with them the person whom he knew to be the principal officer of the customs at Martinsbrück Bridge. He passed on his way, and they continued to pursue theirs. But as Johann jogged on, his thoughts wandered from the cow, and from the various pros and cons respecting the bargain he was about to make for her, to the pertinent question of what these four soldiers with the custom-house officer at their head could possibly be going to Nanders for?

" The moving about of such a party as that," thought he, " can bode no good to any body, and may be, for aught I know to the contrary, as full of mischief as an egg's full of meat;" and thereupon he immediately determined to return home again by the same way he had come, just for the purpose of finding out at Nanders, if possible, where they were going, and what they were about. It was nearly dark, however, before old Bradela got back to Nanders, driving his purchase before him. He had been meditating all day about his encounter of the morning, and lost no time, after safely lodging his cow, before he set off to visit a small wine shop, which he knew was kept by a person in pretty constant correspondence with the Engadin smugglers. To this man he told what he had seen, but he was assured that no such party had made their appearance in Nanders.

It was possible, however, that they might have reached the opening of the gorge into Finstermünz, without having passed through the town, and in fact this was precisely what they would have been likely to do, for the sake of avoiding notice, if their purpose was to in-tercept some convoy of smuggled goods, of the approach of which they had a suspicion. The man to whom Bradela thus told his news was, in fact, the very person to whom Reinhardt's heretical packet was consigned. The good farmer, it must be observed, knew nothing whatever of the affair, but no sooner had the man to whom he recounted his adventure of the morning, heard of the posse he described, than he became greatly alarmed. He had little doubt that the official gentry had somehow or other got scent of the business that was on foot, and that these men were sent to catch the smuggler at the spot where the river emerges into the Austrian territory.

His first idea was to hurry forward himself,

in order to meet Conrad before he should reach the frontier, and to turn him back. But the reflection, that he was himself well known to the revenue officers, that, moreover, he could hardly hope to proceed unnoticed by the party which now occupied the pass, and that his being seen there would very dangerously increase the suspicions which already attached to him, and his calling, by drawing the attention of this party upon him; caused him to abandon the idea of making any such effort, and to content himself by telling the farmer that there could be no possible doubt that the party he had seen were sent out to intercept some poor devil who was labouring to earn an honest penny by braving the blustering blast of that dark night, and that if he happened to fall in with any such, he would be doing a truly Christian office by giving them warning that they were watched.

Johann Bradela readily promised that he would do so, and having rejoined his cow, he set off on his way home. On entering the Finstermünz gorge, he again saw the officer, and one of the four men whom he had met in the morning, and not a shadow of doubt was then left on his mind respecting the nature of their business there.   Johann Bradela, however, reached home without meeting with any one on whom to bestow the warning which he was carrying in his heart.   It was, as I have already said, a very stormy night; the wind was rising, the thunder growled at intervals, and everything seemed to promise what sailors call a dirty night.   Bradela's first care on crossing his own threshold, even before speaking of his new purchase, was to tell his wife and daughter what he had seen and heard about the revenue men, and to say that they must keep a sharp look-out, so as not to let any honest free-trading Swiss fall into the hands of the Philistines for want of a friendly warning.

Poor Ida! what a leap her heart made! and how all her blood at once seemed to rush into her face, and back again the next moment to her heart, leaving her as pale as ashes!

She had said nothing to her father about Conrad's expected coming that night.   Not, indeed, that it was any great secret, for their attachment was no secret, being well known, and well approved both by father and mother, but though she had not talked of their intended meeting, she had thought of little else since the time it was settled, and had been feeding her fancy with meditations on the interview, which despite the storm, she had promised herself, at some little distance from the cottage. Some maidenly shyness had prevented her mentioning this intended meeting before, but now she told her father that Conrad was coming through the pass that night with an important cargo— that no doubt information of his enterprise had reached the officer at Martinsbrück, and that it was a great mercy that he had thus fortunately become acquainted with the fact. Before she had said all this, a cloak and hood were already wrapped about her head and shoulders, in preparation for the sortie that was to take her to meet her lover with the important tidings.

It was by this time near the hour at which she expected him, so without more delay she stepped out into the darkness of the night, and advanced cautiously in the direction of Martinsbrück. There was no reason for her proceeding far, and indeed, as he might have been well trusted as to the not passing the cottage without calling there, it was hardly necessary for Ida to have braved the inclemency of the night at all. But for some reason or other she did not take this rational view of the case, but stepped along her dangerous path with as little fear or care for the rage of the elements as if she were taking a pleasant summer evening's walk by moonlight. At no great distance from the cottage, she met him whom she came out to seek. He advanced stoutly and cheerily along, with a firm step, and an easy, swinging gait, notwithstanding the blustering of the wind, the darkness of the night, the nature of the path, or the heavy burden bound upon his shoulders.

"Ida! darling!" he cried, as soon as he caught a dim sight of her through the darkness and the storm. "I *almost* thought, dearest, that you would not have come out to meet me this night, it is so very rough and blustering, and altogether as ugly a night, my Ida, as ever a smuggler could wish for."

"But you did not *quite* think I should not come, did you, Conrad?" responded his mistress, tenderly. " But now, dearest Conrad, you must listen to me, for I have that to tell which it is most needful that you should hear."

" Do I not always listen to you, my own sweet love? And is not every thing you say important to me, Ida?"

" Nay, but, dear Conrad," returned Ida, gravely, " what I have now to speak is indeed important. My father went to Noberts this morning, and has ascertained, beyond the possibility of doubt, that the revenue officers are on the look-out at the entrance of the pass. They must have got some hint about your plans, dearest Conrad, but they shall have a cold night's watching to small purpose. Was not my father's journey a lucky one to-day?—— But come, dear Conrad, come to our cottage; a good fire, and a warm welcome, are waiting for you there, and you can take your walk to Nanders as soon as we shall be sure that the path is clear."

Thus did the fond, fair Ida, set forth her little scheme; and it must be owned that the temptation to close with it was felt to be strong by Conrad. Not, indeed, that the bold smuggler cared enough about wind and weather to make him anxious to escape from the task before him, for the sake of warm and comfortable quarters; but there were other considerations which certainly did prompt him to put off the execution of his task to a more propitious opportunity; and the thought of turning down the little path which led to the cottage, and towards which Ida's arm, already placed within his own, was most persuasively drawing him, did tempt him strongly. But, no; there were other considerations, which, after a moment's struggle, prevailed with Reinhardt, and made him resist the pleasanter, and pursue the more difficult course.

Could he, in short, make up his mind to be absent from the fête at Schnols, and yield such a triumph to Carl Levette? Could he endure this after what had passed between them on the preceding day? Ida, it is true, would at the least hint of this feeling have willingly absented herself from the fête, and thus, at least, have balked Levette of the promised dance; but could he stoop to such mean means as these in order to extricate himself from the conse-

quences of the promise which he had so boast-
fully led Ida to make? No; he could not do
it: the thing was impossible; and he therefore
resolutely decided upon persevering in his
attempt to carry his cargo through, despite all
the revenue officers in the Tyrol. But how
should he set about it? To proceed by the
pass which he knew to be occupied by five
armed men would be sheer insanity. He
might as well give himself up at once.

Only one other mode of proceeding was open
to him; there was another way—path it was
not, even for a goat—and this way was a tremendous one. After a few moments of self-
concentrated deliberation, Conrad determined
to attempt this desperate mode of passing the
Austrian frontier. The attempt was a remarkable instance both of steadfast courage and of
steadfast will. It consisted in descending from
the spot where he stood, to the river, crossing
it, and then scaling the wall-precipice which
formed the other side of the gorge. To get
down to the river, and even to cross it, was
nothing very difficult, at least in the judgment
of one born and bred amid mountains, rocks,

and torrents, and accustomed to climb, scale, and cross them in every direction. The difficulties of the task would commence when he should have reached the other side. They were not unknown difficulties, however. Conrad knew the cliff well, and had, indeed, scaled it some years before; but it was in the character of a sportsman, and not in that of a smuggler. He had done it in fine weather, by daylight, and with no burthen to carry, except his fowling-piece. To perform the same feat in the profound darkness of a tremendously stormy night, and with a heavy load on his shoulders, was a very different matter. But his resolution was taken to attemp it.

In reply, therefore, to Ida's affectionate pleadings in favour of his abandoning his enterprise for that night, he only said—" Ah, Ida, you tempt me sorely to forget business till to-morrow! But 'Work first, and play afterwards,' is a good saying. Besides, you forget that if I do not get to Nanders to-night, I cannot be at the fête at Schnols to-morrow afternoon. And if I am not there, you know the penalty—Carl Levette will not

forget to exact it. Shall I let him have his
will, Ida?"

"I am sure, Conrad, if you are not at
Schnols, I shall not be there either," said Ida,
with a little sigh. "But what is the use of
talking of such matters when serious affairs
are in question?"

"As to your staying away from the fête,
Ida, it is impossible, because it would be
breaking your promise to Levette, you know,
and a pretty tale he would make of it. And
as to serious affairs, darling, I know of no
affairs that would be so serious to me as the
skulking about these hills to-morrow afternoon,
while Carl was dancing away with you at
Schnols. And the use of talking about it is to
tell you, my own Ida, that I mean to carry
my goods to Nanders to-night, keep tryste at
Schnols to-morrow, and make Carl and all the
rest look yellow with envy at seeing me dance
with the prettiest girl there. And now, darling, you must help me across the river, in
your father's boat, without more loss of time."

"Conrad! dear Conrad!" returned Ida,
gazing at him in dismay; "you cannot be

serious? you cannot dream of attempting anything so wild? Climb the *Nicolaus-mauer*
with that pack, and in this weather! You
cannot dream of doing it."

" I cannot do it by dreaming, my Ida, that
is quite certain," retorted Conrad; "but to do
it wide awake I most certainly will try. So,
dearest, just step down to the river with me,
and show yourself fit to be a smuggler's wife,
by helping to put me across the river, and
then taking your father's boat back again
to its mooring. We have no time for more
talking, dearest Ida, for the night is getting
on. It must be near midnight."

It was impossible to dissuade Conrad from
the scheme he had thus decided on; so, despite
poor Ida's terrors for her lover's safety, they
scrambled down to the river's brink together,
and stepped into a little boat which was
moored to the bank immediately below Farmer
Bradela's cottage. Conrad stepped into it;
and, as he gave his hand to Ida to assist her in
following him, he desired her to tell the old
folks at the cottage that he should tell them
all about his adventure when he met them at

Schnols to-morrow evening.   He then seized
the little paddle, and, with a few dexterous
strokes, impelled the little bark across the
stream.   It required some skill to do this, for
the river was turbulent and swollen, and the
current very rapid.   But neither of the lovers
seemed to consider this as a species of difficulty
worthy of being accounted such.

The stream was passed, the boat touched
the Austrian bank, and Conrad, eager to be on
shore, and off on his journey, tossed the paddle
from his hand and sprang to the bank, holding
firmly the rope by which the boat had been
moored.   As ill luck would have it, the paddle,
in falling from his hand, went overboard, and
was carried away by the stream in a moment,
before either of them could make an effort to
recover it.

" That is unlucky!" cried Conrad.   " How
are you to go back, Ida?   Here, step on shore,
and hold the boat for a moment, till I can cut
you a stick from some of these trees, long
enough to serve you as a paddle."

Ida did as she was bidden; but in taking
the rope from his hand, owing either to his

too great hurry, or her own, she failed to clutch it, and it slipped from both their hands into the water. In a moment the boat was utterly out of reach, whirling away down the headlong current. The position of the lovers now became seriously embarrassing. What were they to do? Passage on that side of the river, either up the stream or down it, for more than a few hundred yards either way, was utterly impracticable. The spot on which they had landed was one of those small flat green bits of alluvial soil, surrounded on all sides by precipitous cliffs, which are often found beside rivers under similar circumstances, being formed by some opposing headland meeting the current, and causing it to deposit there the earthy materials which it bears along with it. It was partially covered with trees, while the cliffs which walled it in were for the most part bare. At the lower end of it, a little torrent fell into the river with much rapidity and noise, greatly increased at that moment by the heavy rain which had fallen during the last few hours.

This little *bach*, as the mountain torrents

are termed in this country, had, in the course
of ages, dug for itself a deep channel in the
face of the rocky precipice, down which it
leaped and bounded into the Inn; and it was
this channel which afforded the sort of goat's
path that rendered it possible for an active
man to scramble up the side of the mountain,
without the absolute certainty of breaking his
neck. And this was the track of which Conrad intended to avail himself. And now that
the reader understands the local position of
the lovers, he will feel the difficulty of giving
any satisfactory reply to the question, " What
were they to do ?"

In truth, their situation was a cruel one,
and the whole difficulty of it was apparent to
Conrad in a moment. The river, swollen by
the recent rains and furiously foaming
forward on its downward course, would have
been crossed with the greatest difficulty, if at
all, by the most practical and athletic swimmer in the world. To imagine it possible to
bear a second person to the other bank, and
that a female, was totally out of the question.

To make their cries heard at Bradela's cottage, amidst the rushing of the waters and the howling of the winds, was equally impossible. To remain where they were till day-light and more moderate weather should give them some chance of making their situation known to the Bradela family, miserable and discouraging as such a course was, seemed to be their only alternative. But to this Ida would not consent. Conrad had been positive and unyielding in the first part of their ill-starred expedition, and it was now Ida's turn to insist: Conrad strongly urged their remaining where they were till the morning; but Ida answered that he would then lose all that he had wished so much to gain—that he would lose it by her carelessness in letting the rope escape from her hand—that she was quite as well able to climb the precipice without a burden, as he was to do it laden with his pack—that she should perish from cold and wet before morning if they remained in inaction where they were— and, finally, that she was determined to proceed with him.

Perhaps Conrad remembered the pithy old adage anent a woman's resolve—

" If she will, she will, you may depend on't
And if she wont, she wont, and there's an end on't."

And, moreover, it could not be denied that two of her arguments, at least, had reason in them. It was not to be denied that they would have had much ado to keep body and soul together till the morning, remaining where they were. And, moreover, Conrad felt that his active Ida was not far wrong in asserting that she could climb the mountain without any burden to impede her, pretty nearly as well as he could do it, laden as he was. The path, if path it could be called, was, to be sure, such as a lowland girl would have deemed about as practicable as a church steeple; but Ida was a mountain lass, and almost as sure-footed as one of her own goats. Then two are always better for such an undertaking than one; help, of the most important description, may be mutually given—in short, Ida prevailed.

The little council of war was brought to a

conclusion, and the determination adopted that both should attempt the ascent of the precipice together—that, being arrived at the top, Conrad should pursue his way across the forest to Nanders, which, if they had luck in their attempt, he might still reach before daylight, while Ida could easily reach the bridge of Martinsbrück, which she might cross without exciting any suspicion, and so be at home to relieve the anxiety of her parents by breakfast time. Such was the plan of their campaign, and no more time was lost ere they began to put it in execution. The swollen condition of the torrent whose channel was to serve them for a path, considerably increased the difficulties of the enterprise, but the real dangers of such an achievement are not exactly what they appear to those unaccustomed to such scenes. The deficiencies of brain and mind are more to be feared than those of limb and muscle. The human foot and arm will bear the human form in safety, if their efforts be not paralysed by weakness of nerve. The sleep-walker will traverse a narrow beam suspended over an abyss, in safety.

They commenced their task with good heart, Conrad leading the way, and turning at each instant, now to indicate the exact spot where he had found it possible to place a foot, now to give a sustaining hand, and again to bend down some tall twig of the brushwood which skirted that part of the torrent, till it was within the grasp of Ida's hand, and might serve as a means of pulling herself up the more precipitous points of the ascent. In this manner they had already attained a considerable height, and had left the foaming river far enough below to have turned giddy the brain of a lowlander by merely thinking of the depth beneath him, when a sudden cry from the other side of the torrent they were ascending caused them both to start. The swiftly careering clouds parted, from time to time, permitting as it were a flash of starlight to pierce through the darkness, and such a chance as this permitted them to descry the dim forms of three men on the other side of the gully, and a little higher up the precipice. They were descending it cautiously and warily, and either by the ear or the eye, had become

aware of the vicinity of our friends a few
minutes before they had themselves been perceived. Conrad felt not a moment's uncertainty as to the business of the strangers.
Who but a smuggler, or a smuggler's *lawful
foe* could be in such a spot at such a time?
He had no doubt but that the three men were
the same whom old Bradela had seen in the
midst of the pass. But what had induced
them to desert their post there, or have led
them to guess his change of course and plans,
was a mystery far beyond his power of
guessing?

He was not, however, long left to mere conjecture on these points, for the strangers had
now descended to a level with him, and were
close enough to be easily seen and heard, notwithstanding the darkness of the night and
the brawling of the torrent. The three men
were now standing on a mass of rock which
had at some former period fallen from the cliff
above, and which afforded them a flat platform
on which they stood commodiously enough.
The narrow gully, down which the torrent
leaped, was between them and the smuggler;

it was impassable at that particular spot, but might be crossed easily enough a few yards higher. Ida was a little way behind Conrad, and consequently somewhat lower down the precipice, so that the overhanging rock on which the revenue officers stood effectually concealed her from their sight.

The parties were thus situated, when the foremost of the three men hailed Conrad, and bade him surrender himself as their prisoner, adding, that the next time he crossed running water while they were on the look out for him, he had better not let his boat float down the stream to carry the tidings.

This was in fact the case. The officers were of course as well aware of the existence of a pass up the side of the Nicolaus-Mauer, possible, though desperately difficult, as the smuggler was; and when one of their number observed an empty boat, floating down the stream at the opening of the gorge, that cir-cumstance, connected with the non-appearance of the person they were waiting for, led them easily enough to surmise the real state of the case.

Poor Ida! It is not very difficult to guess what her feelings must have been when she heard the challenge of the officer, and the taunt which followed it. It was, then, her carelessness which had put the officers on their track! Had it not been for her, all would have gone well! Poor Ida!

It was indeed an awful moment. The officers had firearms, and he who had hailed Reinhardt had, as he did so, levelled his piece at him. Conrad was also armed, but in an exchange of shots, it would have been three to one against him. A moment's consideration sufficed to decide the young smuggler as to the course he should pursue. If there must be a death-struggle between them, he thought his chance would be better were he placed beside his enemies on the platform. His chance would be better in a hand to hand encounter. There was the precipice—as deadly a weapon as the pistol. He therefore, having made a sign to Ida that she was to keep back where she was, out of sight, replied to the challenger that he surrendered, and would come across to them; and having said so, he proceeded for a

few yards to ascend the torrent, till he reached
the spot where it was practicable to cross it,
while the officer, turning as he moved, continued to cover him with his pistol.

The eyes of the three custom-house men
were, as may easily be imagined, all on him,
as he proceeded to cross to their side of the
torrent. It was an interval of breathless sus-
pense! Five minutes might perhaps suffice
Conrad for climbing to the fordable spot, and
for descending again, till he should reach the
platform. In less time it was scarcely possible
to do it; for though the distance was but
trifling, it was difficult ground, and could not
be traversed without considerable caution.
These five minutes were not wasted by Ida.
Her plan of operations had been as quickly
decided upon as that of Conrad. It was the
custom of the young smuggler to carry with
him on all his mountain expeditions a stout
staff, shod with an iron spike. On the present
occasion he had lent this to Ida, to assist her
ascent, and it was in her hand when they
were surprised by the officers. By the aid of
this staff she quickly scrambled down to the

brink of the torrent, and contrived to catch
hold of a long pendent bough of a tree which
grew on the opposite side, immediately below
the mass of rock on which the officers stood.
Taking firm hold of this, she sprang towards
the other bank, and though she fell short of
it, and was plunged into the water, she finally
succeeded in dragging herself out exactly at
the base of the fragment of rock so often mentioned. This fragment of rock, as she had
plainly perceived from the other side of the
gully, rested for support almost entirely on a
smaller mass below, which was itself supported
in the position it had taken by a quantity of
loose stones and earth, which the swollen torrent had already in part washed away.

Very little assistance was wanted, and such
as might easily be given by an active and
willing hand, in order to dislodge the smaller
rock. Great, however, was the risk which any
one who made such an attempt must run of
being overwhelmed by the fall of the huge
mass above. And very fearful, also, was the
thought of thus plunging three human beings
—douaniers although they were—and Aus-

trians to boot—in such certain and terrible
destruction. But ten thousand times more
terrible still was the sickening possibility that
the awful catastrophe might be brought about
a moment too late, and thereby involve in its
destruction the beloved being whom it was
intended to save! But the mind of the young
Ida was strung to the deed. A few desperately
violent strokes of the iron-spiked staff, not given
at random, but at the very weakest point to be
espied at the water-worn base of the smaller
rock, were likely to do much; the instant aid
of the assisting torrent, too, did more than
half the work. The stone quivered as if an
earthquake were busy with it, and then it suddenly gave way and rolled into the abyss. Did
its movement, and the crash which followed it,
make any sound? Who was there that could
tell? It was no noise produced by its headlong plunge into the torrent which to Ida's
ears seemed to make the wind's howling and
the torrent's roar sink into silence; for there
was another and a mightier crash, and there
was a wild cry with it, that would have made
itself distinctly heard to any human ear, though

the mountain itself had fallen. Leaping from
point to point of the jutting cliffs, and thun-
dering as it fell, the fatal platform plunged
into the river below, and left Ida trembling,
shaking in every limb, and almost senseless,
though unharmed, unhurt, though almost, as
it seemed, in the very course over which the
tremendous mass had fallen.

And where was Conrad? One moment
more, and Ida's worst terror would have been
realized! Had her enterprise been achieved
one instant later, she would have been his de-
stroyer instead of his preserver; for he had
been in the very act to spring upon the platform from above, at the moment that the mass
fell, and, with his enemies clinging to it, had
sunk before his eyes into the abyss! He saw
them fall, he heard their despairing cry as they
sunk. The place where they had stood was
there no longer, and below it he saw his Ida
clinging to the boughs which had befriended
her, and scarcely able to stand.

Another moment brought him to her side,
and the true explanation of the catastrophe
nstantly flashed upon him; but as he clasped

her to his bosom, neither of them had power to speak. But their mutual feelings may be guessed at. Ida was dreadfully shaken, more so than her hardy project and stedfast execution of it might have led any one to expect, save those who may have observed how constantly, in women at least, every strong effort of high-wrought resolution is followed by a proportionably violent prostration of both mental and bodily strength.

After a short pause and brief consultation, Ida and her lover resumed their arduous ascent, and succeeded in reaching the summit of the Nicolaus-Mauer in safety.

A very few words will suffice to tell the remainder of the tale. Conrad duly delivered his wares at Nanders, but it was his last trip in the smuggling line. Though Ida had been, somehow or other, beguiled into believing that it was possible a smuggler might do for a lover, nothing could persuade her, after the adventure of that dreadful night, to accept of a smuggling husband. It was impossible. But then she added, that if Conrad could be contented to settle down as a quiet, industrious farmer, she, on her side, could be well contented to be such a farmer's wife; and there was the little farm, which was one day to be all her own; and meanwhile, her parents would be glad that it should be the home of their daughter's husband, the more so that the dear old man would well like to have a stout and active son to help him in the management of it.

But besides a heavy sort of recollection of the tremendous ransom paid for the life of her dear Conrad, which would occasionally cause Ida in after-life to sigh in the midst of great happiness, she carried with her to the grave another mark of that night's sufferings. One long rich lock of her beautiful brown hair had become, before she rose on the following morning, as white as the bosom on which it fell.

*   *   *   *   *   *

" And do you really mean to tell me," said I, to little Martha Weber, who had told the whole story, the horrible death of the revenue officers included, with as much gusto as if she had been relating the shooting of three red deer; "do you really mean to tell me that this is a true story, and that these things happened in your lifetime?"

"No, not in *my* lifetime, *gnädige frau*," returned Bertha, "but in that of my father and mother, and every single word is true, and all remembered by all the old people in the village. But you may have proof if you like it, for at this very moment there are two of Ida's grand-children walking down the road yonder, and sweet pretty creatures they are."

It was impossible to resist the cogency of so conclusive a proof, and I therefore beg that this account of Conrad Reinhardt's adventure may be received as a true and faithful history.

Whether it be so received or not, however, it is, beyond contradiction, characteristic of the locality, and may serve the reader as a memorial of a spot treasured in the remembrance of many travellers.

It may also, perhaps, induce some of those whose wanderings shall hereafter take them to the pass of Finstermünz, not to rest contented with what the high-road can show them of its beauties, but to take the trouble of exploring the far finer and more picturesque gorge which the river traverses between Finstermünz and Martinsbrück.

A MIDNIGHT PASSAGE

OF

THE MONT DU CHAT.

A MIDNIGHT PASSAGE

OF

THE MONT DU CHAT.

———

NOTHING, I suppose, but "a roving disposition" could have tempted me, while the meek
and gentle-looking sun of England was still
looking down with his very best summer smile
upon Ilfracombe—that loveliest of all English
watering-places — nothing else could have
tempted me to turn away, and scamper over
sea and land, for the sake of taking a ramble
among the lakes and mountains of Savoy.
This roving disposition, however, becomes now
and then a pilot that leads one into very pleasant waters; and though I am now going to

narrate an adventure, which certainly might have ended in mischief, I am in no humour, even while relating it, to quarrel with any of the circumstances to which it was owing.

Moreover, it : but justice to the wisdom which originated ι scheme, to declare that nothing could be bettε. 'nagined and better timed for the purpose of indulging my companion and myself in a series of contrasts, exceedingly well calculated to amuse the fancy. Our excursion was, in truth, a succession of shifting scenes, all admirably well calculated to set each other off to advantage.

I have often, in looking about me, while wandering here and there over the pleasantly varied surface of our beautiful earth, amused myself by fancying that there were marked characteristics belonging to the different portions of it, curiously made up of the physical peculiarities of each region, and of the moral peculiarities of its inhabitants. In the " vine-covered hills and gay valleys of France," may one not see a harmony of tone between the land and its indwellers, that proves, almost at a glance, that they were made for each other, and would mutually experience a very melancholy change if they were separated? How could any human being, less good-humoured and easily pleased than a Frenchman, go on from generation to generation, travelling from Paris to Lyons, or to Calais, or to Lisle, or to Strasburg, or to Orleans, or, in short, in any direction you will, and still continue to testify and declare that not any nation of the earth, nor all the nations of the earth put together, can show so picturesque a territory? And what can be so charmingly characteristic as the reasons they bring forward to justify and explain their admiration?

They can see in every closely-trimmed and wearisomely monotonous vineyard, a varied and a brilliant loveliness, that seems to partake of all the wit hereafter to be inspired by the crop it bears. And what can accord better than the rapt, poetic, imaginative temperament of the whole Teutonic race, with the bold, majestic, varied surface of all the lands that speak their tongue? From the towering glacier to the soft valley that nestles at its feet, from the sweeping Danube and abounding Rhine, to the sparkling Moselle and the dancing Inn; from each and all, and from ten thousand thousand other sources equally prolific, may we not trace that boundless variety of thought and of illustration which place our nobly imaginative German cousins on the high intellectual ground they occupy? And does not the heaven of Italy foster still, though silently, all the glowing energy of thought and action which marked it when in health?—and which may mark it yet again ere our globe withers away for ever. And America? Does not the endless continuity of her rivers suggest the " go-ahead" system beyond the power of mistake?

And England, with her temperate clime, and temperately high mountains, and temperately broad rivers, does not her *physique* in all things correspond admirably with her *morale?* Does she not, in all her operations, show herself good at need, and convertible to all utilities? Beautiful *assai*, and immoderate only in wealth and greatness? Yes, yes, all this is too true to be either battled for or controverted, and greatly do such varieties beguile the long journey of life.

And so, after luxuriating for some weeks among the lovely rocks and coves of Ilfracombe, amidst scenery often solemn without being sombre, and noble without being gigantic, the above-mentioned roving disposition sent us off again.

The first thing in the way of comical contrast that occurred to amuse us—to amuse me, I should say, for in this my companion did not share—was furnished by the ladies' style of bathing at Paris. At Ilfracombe there is a deeply-sheltered cove of exquisite beauty, looking so sacredly apart, that it is impossible to enter it without feeling that Diana and her dainty train might there indulge in playing with the cool clear waves for ever, without fearing any audacious hunter's eye, or fisher's either. But how did I find them managing these matters in France?

The lady's bathing-cove at Ilfracombe was such a favourite spot with me, that often, very often, I was wont, though no sea-bather myself, to repair to it, early and late, with some favourite volume in my hand, which rarely, however, succeeded for ten minutes together in withdrawing my eyes from the deep-green sea (with all its battery of rocks) surrounding the delicious basin, for ever ready for the bather's use, and which green sea seemed to be for ever dashing froth and foam into the air, as if Neptune, with a patent artillery of his own, was keeping watch and ward over his fair invaders. And here, in all the mystery of deepest solitude, the daughters of England having once, twice, thrice, perhaps, kissed their native guardian, retreated, with shy step and dripping drapery, each one to her solitary dressing-room, where scarcely a sister's eye was permitted to follow.

It was but a very few days after quitting this most characteristic English bathing-ground, that I found myself, by the invitation of a Parisian friend, in the midst of the lady's swimming-school on the Seine. Never shall I forget the feeling of astonishment which my first glance round its ample enclosure occasioned me!

My friend led me to a bridge that crossed the middle of the enclosure, and from this vantage-ground I looked round, and saw about a hundred figures clothed in little blue *camisoles*, which reached from the throat to the waist, with pantaloons to match. Some were in the water and some out of it; the latter running along the banks of this huge lady-pond, playing a thousand gambols, and from time to time springing with an Undine plunge into the midst of their floating companions— all laughing, all talking, all frolicking,—with the exception of here and there a novice, who was learning the art of swimming in sober earnest, and from whom there occasionally arose a sort of drowning " oh! oh! oh!" as her newly-applied strength failed her, and she found it necessary to call upon the swimming master for aid.

This swimming-master, a quiet, respectable-looking man of thirty-five or forty, appeared to devote himself to one pupil at a time, which, if the pupil happened to be a new one, was quite necessary, as these fair floaters were disporting in water of about twenty feet deep.

He carried a long pole in his hand, with a handle conveniently formed to receive the grasping fingers of the failing water-nymphs.

At the first glance the scene was too grotesque not to produce a laugh; but a second showed a multitude of either pretty, or amusing, or interesting varieties, which soon riveted the attention, and rendered the whole spectacle something that it was exceedingly difficult to cease gazing upon. At one point a group of very young girls, some of them quite children indeed, with an anxious mother or two in the midst, were gazing at each other's queer costume with unbounded merriment, as they stood dallying on the brink, preparatory to taking the plunge.

Some among these pretty little naïads swam like otters; and these, conscious of their power and consequent safety, defied their more timid companions to all sorts of watery gambols. At the head of the inclosure, where the water is deepest, a light flight of steps leads to an elevation of about twenty feet perhaps, and those who feared not to dive, seemed to like nothing so well as the scampering up these steps, and with their slender figures rendered slenderer still by placing their arms as closely as possible in straight lines beside them, letting themselves drop into the water by taking one bold step forward. There was something so exceedingly startling to unaccustomed eyes in thus seeing play and danger mixed together by young girls, with so much reckless daring, that it required some little time to get rid of a feeling of alarm; but when convinced that they were all as safe as if they had been lying on down pillows instead of transparent waves, I began to enjoy the scene exceedingly.

Nothing, perhaps, excites the animal spirits more than a copious ablution in cold water; and this may account for the boundless gaiety with which the majority of these dark-blue mermaids pursued their sport—rolling, tumbling, bounding onwards, darting backwards —now on their breasts, now on their backs, now turning round and round with an agility which, under the circumstances, seemed to me almost miraculous, and now floating so quietly, and with so very little visible exertion, that they seemed intending to take a nap upon their liquid pillows.

As usual in all cases where activity of movement makes the principal point of display, the prettiest part of the performers were the youngest; but, nevertheless, there was one lady who, though decidedly past the age when the *beauté du diable* is so apparent as to eclipse, in some degree, every other charm, was still extremely lovely; and she had, moreover, condescended to bestow a few picturesque touches on her head-gear, having twisted the coloured kerchief which protected her locks from all superfluous moisture, into something of Eastern outline, and very literally turning to "favour and to prettiness," what, in most other instances, had an effect rather unpleasantly the reverse.

This lady was a most accomplished swimmer; but, unlike her juvenile rivals, she displayed not her skill either by springing from on high into the flood, or by diving with dauntless courage till long lost to sight. Neither did she dart with the velocity of

an arrow from one end of the long enclosure to the other. Her feats were not
feats of strength, but of grace; and I was
soon so completely fascinated by her various
beautiful manœuvrings, that I could look at
nothing else. She soon perceived that I was
watching her, and goodhumouredly passed
again, and again, under the bridge on
which I stood, turning up her large lustrous
eyes, and smiling till every bright pearl in the
double row that Nature had given her, seemed
to laugh at me out of the water as she passed.

I very soon became certain that she was in
some way or other a student of attitudes, for
nothing could be more skilful than the manner
in which she contrived to vary the monotony
which her exercise seemed to require. But
though she certainly was taking exercise, and
pretty strong exercise too, I presume, her
movements gave much more the idea of lazy,
voluptuous indolence, than of violent exertion.
She seemed to pillow her head on the water in
a way that no one else did, and turned now
on this side and now on that, and now completely over, with a noiseless slowness of move-

ment, which was rather calculated to suggest
the idea of her doing so to avoid the annoyance
of some rudely-twisted rose-leaf that had crossed
her path, than that she was straining her
muscles to avoid the disagreeable alternative
of being drowned.

Before I left the swimming-school, I learned
that this beautiful swimmer was an actress at
one of the minor theatres. But I believe I
have swum away after all these water-witches
to an immeasurable distance from Savoy and
the Mont du Chat. Wanderers will be wanderers still, whether flourishing their pilgrim's
staff or their gray goose-quill!

Well! The next thing that struck me in
the way of contrast was the bright sky, the
flat fields, and the gay-coloured peasantry of
the Bourbonais, who, in all the pomp and
pageantry of a fair-day, were strutting about
with their indescribable straw-hats stuck on
the top of their heads, grapes in their hands,
and bouquets in their hair.

Every feature of our beauteous Ilfracombe
was so stamped upon my memory, that I had
but to close my eyes, in order to have the

distant picture as distinctly before me as the present one. It was like turning to a bold, cold, severe, and spirit-raising landscape by Salvator, from a warm, snug, glowing, living *copy from Nature*, by Rubens.

Contrast the third was furnished by a travelling companion in the *coupé*. This was a middle-aged French gentleman, sensible, well-informed, obliging, and agreeable.

At the fair we all purchased peaches, and vile things they were, but ripe, and abounding with juice. When our French companion had completed his repast, he deliberately let down a very neat new silk blind (we were travelling by the diligence, the carriage was quite new and very nice), and diligently, for several minutes together, wiped and dried his fingers upon it.

How deep into the moral peculiarities of the two nations may we fairly go to account for the difference of proceeding in such a matter as this? . . . And so we got to Beauvoisin; and there we determined, having twice seen the Pass des Echelles, that we would not see it again this time, but look at the Mont du Chat instead.

That we might set out upon this expedition without losing time on the following morning, we got our baggage examined by the Sardinian authorities overnight, and weary work it was, for unfortunately we had a good many books, all, however, of the most innocent and innoxious kind, but this did not avail us, for they were all seized, as well as a packet or two of writing-paper, of a quality only to be found in Paris, and which was probably taken, not because there was any mischief in it just then, but lest there might be by and by. The whole of the offending articles were put under official seals, and what became of them afterwards we have yet to learn.*

We bore our misfortune as well as we could, and quite forgot it the next morning, when at six o'clock on one of the clearest and sweetest of September mornings, we found ourselves trotting along sideways, in the queerest but most commodious of carriages, well stuffed, upon easy springs, and so near the ground that one might be in and out of it a dozen times in as many minutes, without the driver

* These were all forwarded to us at Florence afterwards.

being consulted on the subject. This facility in the transferring one's person to the spot from whence one most wished to look out, was especially agreeable in a country so surpassingly lovely as that through which we were passing; and I shall ever account my little Savoy "volantin," as this machine is called, with its one horse, its four wheels, and its easily-unhooked little wicket in front of the sidelong seat, as one of the very pleasantest conveyances I ever got into.

We followed the course of the Guiers Vif— so called in contradistinction to the Guiers Mort, which runs near the Grande Chartreuse —to the village of St. Genix, where we breakfasted in a queer little *café*, not in a style sufficiently luxurious to tempt us to the loss of much time. The narrow little valley, often just wide enough, with scarcely an inch to spare, for the river and the "volantin" to run side by side, is very pretty; but it is after passing St. Genix that the beauty of the excursion commences.

Near the village, the Guiers Vif falls into the Rhone, and from that point, the road, following the upward course of the latter river, presents a ceaseless succession of beautiful landscapes. Near the point of junction, a bold suspension-bridge, over the Rhone, with a picturesque castle on a towering height above, both named " le cordon," produces one of those startling landscapes which no eye can contemplate with indifference. The mountain of the Grande Chartreuse is one of the most remarkable points in its majestic back-ground. From this point to the beautifully-situated little town of Yenne, the valley of the Rhone offers a series of pictures that it would be difficult to rival anywhere. On the right, in ascending the river, this valley is bounded by noble limestone cliffs, rising almost perpendicularly from the road. At intervals, however, there are soft and gracious slopes of the richest verdure, varied by a growth of underwood that sometimes assumes the aspect of a forest.

The road often skirts the blue and rapid stream with nothing but a parapet to divide them, but retreats at intervals to leave space for the vast masses of rock which have fallen from the cliffs above. On the other side of the river, the hills rise more gently, and are for the most part cultivated. As the road approaches Yenne, the scenery increases in interest. A French fort, of very imposing appearance, called St. Pierre Châtel, defends the narrow pass, and at its foot the river makes a sharp turn eastward, and is soon found to be issuing forth from a narrow gorge between the mountains. Immediately beneath the fort a suspension-bridge connects Savoy and France, and passing by the foot of this, the road and the river enter the defile together, and have it all to themselves. Had the light of day shone a little less brilliantly above us, or had the days of the mountain banditti been less completely gone and over, this would have been a very pretty spot to get up an adventure in; but now, with all its pretty frowns and picturesque gloominess, it looks like a spot well calculated to frighten fairies, if they chanced to come upon it unexpectedly in a moonlight ramble.

At Yenne we dined, not too luxuriously, and then traversed a few miles of peculiarly rich country, preparatory to beginning the ascent of the Mont du Chat. But all this lovely scenery, had not been passed through *au grand galop*, nor even *au petit trot*, for we had walked very deliberately through great part of it, enjoying heartily a mode of conveyance which enabled us to linger on our road as much as we liked.

It was, I believe, about six o'clock when we quitted Yenne, and as the moon was nearly at the full, we had no doubt of being able to reach Chambéry without having any cause to repent of the delay in which we had indulged. So off we set again, in excellent spirits, and with that delightful species of excitement which is always felt, I believe, at the approach of a celebrated mountain pass, by those to whom the climbing it is as completely a labour of love as it is to me and my companion. It chanced that it was not till our dinner at Yenne was concluded that we remembered the celebrity of one particular species of wine which is the growth of a vineyard in the neighbourhood. We were by no means inclined to delay further our already late departure for the purpose of renewing our dessert with the accompaniment of this *vin d'Altesse*, as it is called, but neither were we willing to omit the opportunity of tasting the only produce of the grape which is thought to resemble champagne, and which has, moreover, the additional interest of owing its existence to the patriotism of a native prince, who brought the first plants that produced it from Cyprus.

We accordingly purchased a flask, and stowed it in a corner of the carriage, being cautioned, however, by the seller, not to leave it there too long, as it was sufficiently *mousseux* in its nature to burst its bonds and descend upon us in a sparkling shower, if we did so. Accordingly our travelling corkscrew and drinking-cups were brought forth as soon as we began the ascent of the mountain. We found the wine very good, very much *up*, and, as it seemed to me, very strong, and, moreover, we agreed that it would have been greatly improved by being *frappé*. However, we each took our cupfull, and then perceiving that the

view was already becoming more splendid, and
the path beside the road in every way inviting,
we determined to walk; but, fearing that our
vehemently *mousseux* wine might play us a
trick in our absence, and cause the dusty little
carriage to undergo a more thorough washing
than we should just then approve, we made
over the flask to the driver, explaining the
reasons for our generosity, and telling him to
do whatever he liked with it, save replacing it
inside the carriage. And then we began to
mount, slowly and luxuriously, in the sweet,
freshening breeze of evening, with a landscape
at our feet that seemed to spread itself wider
and wider as we mounted. But slowly as we
walked, the horse, as it seemed, walked more
slowly still, for we soon left it behind us, and
continued to mount the admirably well-ma-
naged ascent, without giving ourselves a moment's concern for having lost sight of it. The
only living thing we met was a woodcutter,
and this was just at the spot where the brushwood which so richly clothes the lower part of
the mountain begins to vanish by degrees,
giving place to the sharply-pointed, savage-

looking rocks which form the great beacon-point of the neighbourhood. He was driving, very literally driving before him, a small cart filled with wood, which was mounted on four low wheels, and which by the aid of an occasional touch from him, was steadily pursuing its way towards Yenne without the assistance of any horse, ass, ox, or mule, whatever.

After passing this very independently loco-motive machine, the ascent became steeper, and we began to look back the way we had come in the hope of descrying the carriage, for I had just then a notion that being carried for the next mile or so might be still more delightful than walking. But we looked in vain. Still, however, we were not in the least degree alarmed or annoyed; instead of resting by means of the carriage, we reposed ourselves by standing still and gazing on the gorgeous landscape.

The air was so deliciously bright and clear that we never troubled ourselves to decide how much of the silvery light around us proceeded from the sun, and how much from the moon;

had we done this, we should have discovered
that night was very rapidly taking the place
of day, and that it would be quite as well to
be looking after our baggage, as luxuriating in
the splendour of the glorious but fading light
which was spread over the enormous landscape
below. The magnificent terraces of this noble
road were more delightful to me than almost
any I had ever traversed, for they were protected by a parapet, so that, as Rousseau says,
" Cela faisait que je pouvais regarder le fond,
et gagner des vestiges tout à mon aise."

And long did we enjoy the occupation
afforded by hanging over this precious parapet,
and tracing the principal objects of the
country through which we had been travelling; I, with true feminine courage, selected
the spots where the precipice was the most
awfully perpendicular, for the purpose of enjoying the stirring sense of danger, in union
with the comfortable feeling of security—much
as I have seen a little dog barking at a great
one athwart the bars of a lofty gate. The
whole scene was one of great beauty. On one
side, an almost boundless landscape, through

which the Rhone might still be traced, catching the fading light at intervals, and causing here a ruined tower, and there a massive fort, to look mysteriously dark by the contrast. On the other, the road was sometimes skirted by patches of stunted but very picturesque underwood, and sometimes by huge masses of rock, that pierced through the soil, and showed us plainly enough what sort of region we had reached.

To render the effect perfect, the clear voice of a young peasant-girl, driving a score or so of goats before her, broke upon the stillness of this most lovely evening with a sweet, pipe-like purity of tone that was delightful. As she and her goats slowly opened upon us from behind a projecting crag, I caught distinctly a few of the words she was singing, which were remarkable as being neither French nor Italian, but something that seemed to hover between both.

To my great delight I afterwards got hold of an old ballad-sort of thing, at Chambéry, from which I am convinced her morsel was taken. The lines run thus:

" Di bassà Tarantaisa
   Du pay d'ien de s'ai
   Son trè zenti zomò
   Que son amoireu de mèi;
   L'on é le fi d'on conto,
    L'utro é le fi d'on prince,
   Un utro é le fi d'on ré—
   O ché d'amor per mè!"

The watching this girl and her goats, and
the listening to her song, helped very effec-
tively to beguile us of a little more of our
precious time; but when she had quite passed
out of sight and hearing—which, however was
not very speedily, for we watched her vanish
and appear again upon one terrace after another as she descended to the plain—but
when at length we had quite lost sight of her,
we began for the first time to feel seriously
alarmed about our carriage and dinner.

It is so very common an occurrence with
us, when travelling " *vetturino,*" to outwalk
our equipage in mounting a hill, that we were
prepared for considerable delay on so great a
length of up-hill road as we were now traversing; but allowing, with all possible liberality,
for the greatest imaginable slowness, it was
beginning to be very disagreeably evident

that some accident must have happened, for if
the horse had moved at all, he must, we
thought, have moved within sight of us by
that time. What was to be done? I had
enjoyed walking up the mountain exceedingly,
but I was much too tired to feel the least in-
clination for retracing my steps, especially as
I began to think it very doubtful if we should
find our little carriage in a condition to help
us up again. Our situation, now that we
were at length awakened to a consciousness of
it, was really very embarrassing. Whatever was
the cause of the man's delay, it was very important that he should be looked after, for not
only was the whole of our travelling wardrobe
in his hands, but a considerable sum in travelling money also.

"Will you venture to remain here alone,
while I use my best speed to run down the
hill to look for him?" demanded my companion.

There was a good deal of sheer cowardice, I
dare say, in the difficulty which I felt in
giving an answer. Doubtless the mountain's
side was as safe then as it had been an hour

before, when I should very readily have answered
the same question in the affirmative; but no
one can fairly judge of what it seemed to involve at that moment who has not looked
about him a little, exactly at the same spot,
and at a similar hour. Anything more wild
and desolate than this highest part of the pass
can hardly be imagined. It is true that the
moon shone with unclouded brightness; but
although this lovely light was quite sufficient
to prevent my complaining of the darkness, it
rather tended, I think, to increase my idle
fears, than to lessen them; for the heavy
masses of shade thrown by the capriciously-
shaped rocks beneath which I stood, were
really appalling, and there seemed to be more
certainty of total darkness where the moonlight did not come, than of seeing clearly the
objects that reflected it where it did. I bit-
terly regretted that we had not arrived at a
sober comprehension of our position before the
goat-herdess had passed out of sight; for I
doubt not but a few sous would have made
her my willing companion for a little while,
and I could have been perfectly satisfied in

listening to her chantings concerning the " *tre zenti zomò*," for a longer time than would have sufficed my companion to reach the foot of the mountain.   But this bright thought came all to late, and I endeavoured to look braver than I felt as I replied that I was not at all afraid of being left, and that I would either remain where I was or stroll slowly back the way we had come, if he would immediately set off with all speed.

I had hardly uttered the words before I was alone.   And then I began to tell myself how very beautiful the scene before me was, and how very bright the moon that shone upon it, and inwardly made a great many more very sensible observations, all tending to prove that I was exceedingly fortunate in being on so beautiful a spot, and that I might depend upon it that I had the mighty Mont du Chat wholly and solely to myself.   This sort of vapouring did very well for a little while, but by degrees I got exceedingly uncomfortable; the absence of my companion seemed interminable; the shadows appeared to be growing bigger, and the light less.   And then—I became perfectly convinced that I heard the howl of a wolf at no great distance. This settled the matter at once. Had I been certain that walking down the mountain I had walked up would have brought me to climb its lofty side again three times over, I could not have remained where I was; and it was with a feeling of infinite relief that, having thus resolved, I set off on my return down the hill. Walking down an ably-engineered road on the side of a mountain is a very different thing from walking up it; and though I intended to go very slowly, I rather think I did the contrary, for with all my impatience, it appeared to me but a short time before the broad moonlight showed me, on the terrace below that on which I was walking, a group of objects of which the carriage evidently was one. A few minutes more brought me beside I——, who was bending over the body of a man lying by the road-side, to all appearance dead.

That our unfortunate driver had met his fate from some at present inexplicable accident, appeared certain, for the horse had drawn himself and the carriage to a spot by the road-side

where he could contrive to regale himself both
by the leaves and grass of a little copse which
skirted it, and was standing as quietly as a
donkey might have done under similar circumstances. I uttered an exclamation of horror
on perceiving the extended body of the unfortunate man.

"What can we do with him, my dear
I——?" said I, with a convulsive sigh;
"what is to be done with the body?" and I
remembered with a shudder the howl of the
wolves I was so certain of having heard above.

"Do with him?" reiterated my companion;
" we must wake him, if it be possible."

Now, the beams of the moon fell upon the
up-turned face of the man, and I thought he
looked so ghastly pale that I could hardly help
replying—

"Awake the dead!"

I perceived, however, that the quotationwould
be ill-timed, and therefore only said,

" Is he asleep, then?"

" Dead asleep, and dead drunk too, I'm
afraid," was the reply, " and what in the world

we are to do with him, I know not. There
lies the empty flask, you see."

The mystery was now explained; but the
better we understood it, the more embarrassing
did our condition appear, and heartily did I
wish that the patriotic Duke of Savoy had suf-
fered the vines of Cyprus to remain undisturbed
on the soil where nature planted them, instead
of bringing them to corrupt the manners of his
simple Montagnards. Nor was it much consolation to remember that the fault was rather
ours than his. There we were, with all our
belongings, pretty nearly at the top of an
enormous mountain, with no available means
of conveying either ourselves or them to any
inhabited spot of earth; for to march off the
carriage and horse, leaving the owner by the
road-side, would be scarcely honourable, while
every attempt to arouse the said owner to a
sense of his condition, and the performance of
his duty, became every moment more utterly
hopeless. The man snored louder than my
wolves had howled; and there really seemed
no alternative save passing the night in watch-

ing his slumbers, abandoning our property altogether, while we trudged in search of a shelter for ourselves, or setting off, as before hinted, with the carriage and horse.

Now, though our dilemma had thus three horns instead of two, our condition was little the better for it, so difficult was it to decide which was the least objectionable of the three. At length, I had the honour of suggesting the bright idea of depositing the coachman in the vehicle, and patiently walking beside it till we reached a roof under which we might take shelter for the night. It was immediately decided that we should act upon this; but there was something so indescribably absurd in the process we had to go through before we could put it in action, that, despite of our real and genuine distress, we laughed for a few moments very heartily.

But our sedateness soon returned, for, alas! there was a great deal of very heavy work to get through before we could be again *en route*. Fortunately our little Savoyard *ivrogne* was no giant, so the business of rolling him over and over, till he was got to the best spot for hoisting him into the carriage, was less laborious than it might have been; but as this was an operation in which, notwithstanding all my desire to be useful, I could not assist, it was not got through without difficulty. At length, however, he was fairly in the carriage, the door was shut, and off we set. I really am at a loss to imagine anything much more ludicrous than our situation. The moon was now in its very brightest glory over our heads, and we passed round the stern, majestic-looking rock that seems to guard the summit of the pass, at an hour that would have made every step of the marvellously fine descent upon lake Bourget positively sublime, had there not been something in the style and manner of our *cortège* which turned it into a joke. Hardly had we proceeded a hundred yards, however, ere the manner of our march was changed. The soporific qualities of the *Altesse* wine had enabled its victim to withstand bawling, shaking, pulling and rolling, but no sooner did the well-known jingle of his horse's bell and the rattle of his carriage wheels reach his ears, than the mysterious veil which envelops

the faculties in sleep—whether tipsy or sober
—was withdrawn, and ere we had any notice
whatever of what was going to happen, the
man was at our side.

His first stammerings and stutterings were
utterly unintelligible; but by degrees it became evident, that though a good deal puzzled
and confounded, his sound nap had sufficed to
restore his senses sufficiently for him to comprehend that it was his business to drive, and
ours to be driven. I did not, however, immediately relish the idea of trusting ourselves to
his coachmanship, for the road, though admirably constructed, is occasionally steep, and
the tourniquets are sometimes sharp enough
to make it at least seem probable that a carriage may overturn, if twisted round them
incautiously. But I was by this time exceedingly tired of walking, and perceiving that
the poor fellow really looked as sober as a
judge, I got in, though my companion, for my
greater security, retained his station at the
horse's head.

The first perfectly satisfactory proof which
the driver gave me that he was indeed himself

again, was his descending from the box and placing himself at the door of the carriage, in order to point out to my notice the exquisite beauty of the moonlight view. This descent of the Mont du Chat is greatly celebrated for its beauty; but I doubt if those who have only seen it by daylight have any idea how surpassingly lovely it *can* be. Never can I forget the silver lustre of the lake over which the road seemed to hang, or the unspeakable clearness of the black shadows which here and there a towering promontory cast upon it, and the deep stillness, and the soft, sweet air, after a day of intense heat. In short, our adventure was no longer considered as a misfortune; and it was more than once or twice either, notwithstanding all the up-hill and down-hill walking I had had that day, that I again left the little carriage in order to enjoy to perfection the enchantment of the scene.

But when at length the level of the Lac de Bourget is reached, the beauty ceases; for the lake itself becomes invisible, and the mere outline of the mountain tops beyond, although seen through a flood of silver light, could not makè me forget that I had just climbed a mountain higher still. The town of Aix les Bains, which from the mountain side seemed almost close to us, though on the other side of the lake, was now totally out of sight, and the long line of tall poplars beside which we trotted wearily along toward Chambéry, seemed endless. Welcome were the lights which were still visible, *ça et là*, in this remote little metropolis, and more than half asleep was I when, at length, we stopped at *Le Post*, which is the principal hotel in the city. It was a sore trial of our philosophy to be told at such a moment that there was not a chamber vacant! But it had to be borne; and we did bear it with a very considerable degree of magnanimity, considering the number of hours which had elapsed since we had left our last bed, and all that had been done in the interval. But we were speedily rewarded; for at the *Hôtel de l'Europe* we found exactly everything we wanted, and I was soon as sound asleep as if I too had emptied a flask of *vin d'Altesse*.

A VISIT

TO

ROUSSEAU'S FAVOURITE RESIDENCE,

LES CHARMETTES.

A VISIT

TO

ROUSSEAU'S FAVOURITE RESIDENCE,

LES CHARMETTES.

"Le nom d'un écrivain qui exalta si vivement les âmes est réclamé par l'histoire. En s'occupant de Rousseau, elle perd son impossibilité ; et tour à tour elle l'admire ou le plaint, le bénit ou l'accuse."—LACRETELLE *le jeune.*

THOSE who drive post through Chambéry, *ventre à terre*, commit an injustice towards Savoy, and great unkindness towards themselves, provided, that is to say, they are furnished with an average portion of the power of deriving enjoyment from fine scenery, which is providentially bestowed upon mortals, in order to render agreeable their wanderings over the craggy globe assigned to them as the

R 2

locale of their mortal pilgrimage. To all such,
the neighbourhood of Chambéry is calculated
to afford great delight; and for the happy few
who have at will the power of devoting the
months of summer to rambling, I think it
would be difficult to find a more judicious spot
for their head-quarters. Nay, such as are not
mere summer ramblers, but who set off from
their homes with the important object of a
long journey before them, " un voyage à faire,
et Naples au bout," would do well to pause
among the mountains and lakes of Savoy, for
they will find nothing of the same tone amidst
the sunny glories of Italy. I give this counsel
with the more confidence, because I have practised what I preach, and that so recently, as
to have all the benefits derived from it fresh
upon my memory.

Being *en route* for Italy, and having an
idle week or two of certain fine weather to
spare, we devoted the brightest days of last
September to wandering among the Alps of
Savoy, leaving Chambéry for a day or two at
a time, and returning to it again and again,
as the centre from which every excursion

could most conveniently be made. And for many of these there was no need to leave our comfortable hotel at Chambéry at all, for there are many which, by means of early rising, may be brought within the compass of a day; and others—by no means the least interesting— which may be achieved in an hour or two.

Among these last, a visit to Les Charmettes must of course rank first; for there are few persons, I think, who could fail to feel an interest in visiting the spot on which Jean-Jacques declares himself to have passed the happiest portion of his generally unhappy existence.

Perhaps no man ever died, leaving so much that was immortal behind him for the examination and judgment of mankind, on whom sentence has been passed so variously. In the course of my life I have listened to opinions respecting Rousseau, which have graduated from the deepest execration to admiration the most enthusiastic; and not admiration only, for that is a feeling not unfrequently elicited by beings we detest; but I have heard many, and good men too, declare that there were qualities of heart and soul in Rousseau which could not be contemplated without reverence and love; while others—and these others, certainly good men also—shudder as they hear his name, and seem truly and honestly to believe that if there be a case on record in which that most beneficent command, " JUDGE NOT," may be set aside with impunity, it is his; and that the consigning him to everlasting condemnation must, of necessity, be considered as an act of piety in the consigner.

That there are a multitude of human beings, both in times present and times past, whose characters are, and have been, more easily mistaken than understood, is very certain, and is a fact too potent to require or permit of discussion.   But that a voluminous writer—and one, too, who has laid himself and his actions bare, with a degree of unshrinking and unscrupulous audacity that no other individual ever approached—that such an one should so completely have set man's judgment at fault in attempting to understand him, is strange. The solution of the enigma must be sought, and may, as I think, be found, at the same source from whence arises its intricacy.

The critic, from his chair of authority, and the general reader, from his lounging sofa, have both been accustomed to look at men, through their writings, with a sort of habitual allowance for any little egotistical flights in which they may have represented themselves too much *en beau*, but are quite unused to the process necessary for detecting egotistical exaggeration in an opposite direction. But to judge Rousseau fairly, this must be done. It is quite evident that the genius of this celebrated man, though of a nature to elevate him perpetually into the very highest regions of intellectual sublimity, was accompanied by a weakness of character, which, displayed as it is, by way of self-discipline and atonement, in the pages of his Confessions, places him often as much below the ordinary dignity of human nature, as many of his speculations lead us to place him above it. Those on whom these speculations produce a deeper effect than do his penitential anecdotes, are perhaps somewhat too apt to forget altogether the latter; and of such is composed the by no means small troop of his admirers; while, on the other hand, those whose memory retains more vividly the anecdotes than the speculations, naturally fall into the other extreme, and consider him almost as a monster.

As this latter judgment cannot be uttered but in a tone of indignant and outraged morality,—for which, Heaven knows, the unhappy philosopher gave frightful cause,—it has naturally followed that a very large proportion of such as have deemed him more weak than wicked have shrunk from saying so, lest such a judgment should be mistaken for a proof of lax morality in themselves: and thus the suffrages of those who have really made themselves acquainted with his works have perhaps never yet been fairly counted.

It has often been said, and at the first glance, indeed, very plausibly, that the character of a man may be more fairly judged by a history of his actions than by a history of his thoughts. But without examining the possible fallacy of this, in many instances, it must be evident to those who will study, with a little care, the portrait of himself which this great writer has left us, that, in his case at least, such fallacy is undeniable. All that was great and good in the heart and soul of Rousseau was indigenous, innate, born with him, and formed the real and essential material of his character; while all that was bad, degraded, and vile, arose from the miserable associations into which he was unhappily thrown at the most important moment of his existence.

When, before he had reached the age of sixteen, Jean-Jacques ran away from his native town, in order to escape the savage treatment which he knew he should receive from the hands of his brutal master (for having made a Sunday evening ramble into the country so long as to render it impossible for him and his joyous companions to return till half an hour after the gates of the town were shut)—when he thus rushed upon the world, leaving every thing like safety and protection behind him, he carried with him as innocent and affectionate a heart as Nature ever gave; and had he then been so blessed by chance as to have fallen into virtuous hands, there is every reason to believe that his career would have been as happy and respectable as it was lamentably the reverse.

It would be difficult, I think, to find, in any autobiography extant, a passage of more pathos, or of more self-evident truth, than that in which the unhappy man laments the circumstances which made him what he was, and which tore him from what he might have been. After speaking of the position he should have probably held as an engraver in his native town, he goes on to say,

" Si j'étais tombé dans les mains d'un meilleur maître, j'aurais passé, dans le sein de ma religion, de ma patrie, de ma famille, et de mes amis, une vie paisible et douce, telle qu'il la faillait à mon caractère, dans l'uniformité d'un travail de mon goùt, et d'une société selon mon cœur. J'aurais été bon chrétien, bon citoyen, bon père de famille, bon ami, bon ouvrier, bon homme en toute chose. J'aurais aimé mon état, je l'aurais honoré peut-être; et après avoir passé une vie obscure et simple, mais égale et douce, je serais mort paisiblement, dans le sein des miens. Au lieu du cela—quel tableau vais-je faire?"*

---

* " If I had fallen into the hands of a better master, I should have passed a peaceful and gentle life, such as my character

It would be difficult, I think, to read this without prejudice, and not to mourn over the faults of the writer, rather than execrate them. The passage, however, is not without its moral use; it was written after the author had enjoyed all the gratification that an enormous literary fame could bring him, in Paris and in London, personally among the most distinguished individuals in both, and throughout Europe by the scarcely less gratifying sensation produced among all orders of reading men by his works; a gratification not likely to be much lessened by the fact, that among the multitudes who read his theories, no small number thought themselves called upon to abuse him for them. Jean-Jacques, with all his fantastical attachment to his own notions,

required, in the bosom of my religion, of my country, of my family, and my friends, in the routine of an employment which suited my taste, and of a society which suited my heart. I should have been a good Christian, a good citizen, a good father, a good friend, a good workman, a good man in every way. I should have loved my profession, and might perhaps have done honour to it; and, after having passed a life obscure and simple, but tranquil and serene, I should have died peacefully in the bosom of my own people. Instead of this—what is the picture I am about to trace?"

whether right or wrong, would probably have been extremely mortified had no one thought his startling speculations of sufficient importance to provoke hostility from those against whose systems they were aimed. But it is evident, from the passage above cited, written towards the close of his melancholy life, that not all the fame which had succeeded to the obscurity of his early years, had sufficed to atone to his spirit for having lost, in the tumult of his passions, the precious treasure of his own esteem. There is the essence of many an excellent sermon in this. Nor is this the only valuable lesson to be extracted from the study of Rousseau. Whatever were his faults, that of accusing others in order to exculpate himself is not among them. On the contrary, he falls so violently into the other extreme, that it requires all the intuitive and irresistible conviction of his sincerity, which all his disclosures carry with them, to enable one to believe that he is in earnest when he calls his negligent father *un père excellent*, and that detestable source of all his deepest moral corruption, Madame de Warens,

la meilleure des femmes. Now it must be
evident, I think, to any one who reads the
early part of the Confessions, that had this *père
excellent* done his duty by his motherless boy,
that boy would never have had such confessions to make. In the first place he tells us,
that when he was seven years old, he used to
keep him up reading romances, aloud and alter-
nately, till *entendant le matin les hirondelles,*
he sent him to bed, saying, "*allons nous
coucher—je suis plus enfant que toi.*" Of
the nature of these romances it is not difficult
to judge, as Rousseau says, "J'acquis par cette
dangereuse méthode une intelligence unique à
mon âge sur les passions."

They had read through the collection which
his mother, who died at his birth, had left
behind her, in 1719. Jean-Jacques was born in
1712, and the lasting mischief produced by
these baby studies may be traced almost
through every page of these strange volumes
—strange, and often disgusting, despite the
unequalled beauty of the style, and the still
more captivating freshness of original thought,
and occasional good feeling, which may be found

scattered through their pages. When the unhappy boy ran from Geneva, to escape the
anticipated anger of the master engraver to
whom he had been bound apprentice, it seems
that his father rode after him, but did not
overtake him. They reached the house of
Madame de Warens, however, but not till the
poor boy had been sent on to Turin, for the
purpose of being converted to the Roman
Catholic faith. Notwithstanding his unceas-
ing protestations that his father was one of
the best of men, he permits himself to say,
when speaking of this tardy pursuit by this
good father, and the friend who accompanied
him, " Ils se contentèrent de pleurer mon sort
avec Madame de Warens, au lieu de me suivre
et de m'atteindre, comme ils l'auraient pu
facilement, étant à cheval et moi à pied; il
m'aimait très tendrement, mais il aimait aussi
ses plaisirs."

Moreover, considering that this " tender
father" had married a second wife, and kept
possession of the little fortune which Jean-
Jacques inherited from his mother, it is difficult to give him credit for the *probité sûre*

which his son attributes to him.   The idea
of remaining in possession of the poor destitute wanderer's little fortune during his absence, says Jean-Jacques, "ne s'offrait pas à
lui directement; mais elle agissait sourde-
ment, sans qu'il s'en aperçût lui-même. Voila,
je crois," he adds, " pourquoi, venu à Annecy
sur mes traces, il ne me suivit pas jusqu'à
Chambéri, où il était moralement sûr de
m'atteindre."   He follows this vainly pal-
liated statement of unnatural and most criminal neglect, by remarking, that it is always
dangerous to place our duties and interests in
opposition ; and says, by way of complete
apology and excuse, that a person, when so
circumstanced, " devient injuste et méchant
dans le fait, sans avoir cessé d'être juste et
bon dans l'âme."

I know no instance, throughout these painful volumes, in which his own faults are thus
gently treated.   But if his indulgence towards
this very unnatural father, whose negligence
was unquestionably the primal source of all
his faults and misfortunes, is carried to an
absurd excess, the reiterated expressions of

admiration and esteem for Madame de Warens, which he evidently makes it a point of duty to repeat on every possible occasion throughout his life, appears to me to savour of absolute madness. As far as my reading and my memory enable me to judge, the character and conduct of this woman are as detestable as any on record. She was not, indeed, guilty of any crimes of violence, her temper not being of the quality which inclined her to it; but it is scarcely unfair to say that, had this accident in her organization been different, her conduct, in this respect, would have been different also; for assuredly she has left us no reason to suppose that principle would have restrained her. Had the wretched boy who found in her detestable blandishments such a contrast to the ill usage of his brutal master as bewildered his judgment for life—had he, throughout the whole of his melancholy record, persevered in painting her as amiable, despite the hateful qualities which his perverted judgment overlooked, or excused; his ceaseless protestations of unbounded and most exalted esteem, though not likely to produce more

sympathy, would at least have created less astonishment. But when we find him relating anecdotes of her depravity, of which he was himself
the victim, and acknowledging that he was so,
his persevering praise looks like the morbid
timidity of a conscience that finds relief both
in unmeasured self-reprobation, and equally
unmeasured charity, for kindred sins in others;
and, while admiring the majestic strength of
his indignation against those whose faults
have very decidedly no analogy with his own,
it is difficult not to remember that men
have been known to fancy that they might
atone—

> " —— for faults they are inclined to,
>   By damning those they have no mind to."

Yet it is scarcely fair, perhaps, to say this,
after reading the passage in which he re-
proaches himself, with such evidently deep
sincerity, for not having devoted himself to
this utterly depraved woman during the latter
years of her life. He *did*, as it seems, im-
plore her most earnestly to take up her abode
with him in Paris, when she had so involved
her affairs as to have scarcely the means of

existence left; but this she refused, probably preferring the life she was leading at home. But it was upon seeing her when she was between fifty and sixty years of age, upon occasion of his making a visit to Geneva, that he committed the unpardonable crime, as he appears to consider it, of not remaining with her.

He says of this meeting, " Je la revis; dans quel état, mon Dieu ! *Quel avilissement!* Que lui restait-il de sa vertu première?" So that no delusion seems at that moment to have bewildered his judgment concerning her. Yet, notwithstanding her acknowledged *avilissement*, he perseveres in declaring her to have been altogether the most admirable person in the world. He exclaims, *à propos* of this state of *avilissement*, " Ah! c'était alors le moment d'acquitter ma dette" (his debt!!!) Il fallait tout quitter pour la suivre, m'attacher à elle jusqu'à sa dernière heure, et partager son sort, quel qu'il fut. Je n'en fit rien. Je gémis sur elle, et ne la suivis pas. De tous les remords que j'ai sentis de ma vie, voilà le plus vif, et le plus permanent."

Now considering that this woman had thrown him off, in the most unfeeling manner, about fifteen years before, when he was perfectly destitute, and most devotedly attached to her, and this for the sake of a young hairdresser whom she had somehow or other picked up during a short absence of Rousseau from her farm, (the management of which appears to have been his ostensible employment)—considering that such was the cause and manner of their separation, those poignant regrets for not having devoted his life to her when they (almost accidentally) met again, really looks either like hypocrisy or madness. Nobody, I conceive, can believe it to be the first, who has read his true, his terribly true autobiography; and it would be equally impossible to charge seriously with madness, the most powerful and eloquent writer of his day. But it is easier to reject both madness and hypocrisy, as the causes of this strangely perverted judgment of an abandoned woman, concerning whose actions he was in no degree deceived, than to assign any other.

The only theory on the subject that I can

suggest is, that from almost his earliest infancy, his moral sense was confused, bewildered, and depraved. What with his romances, his *homme de plaisir* for his *père excellent*, and Madame de Warens for his instructress, from the age of fifteen to five-and-twenty, he literally and *honestly* ceased to know right from wrong on many points; and having an extremely warm, gentle, and affectionate heart, he was unable to resist the slightest appearance of kindness; so that it was quite sufficient, in order to secure his unbounded esteem, that either men or women should persuade him of their affection for himself.

There was probably a strong mixture of vanity, as well as of tenderness, in this weakness; and his constitutional shyness, which rendered all demonstration of partiality more than commonly precious to his sensitive and timid self-love, left him totally incapable of passing a sane judgment on the real worth of any one who appeared to like or love him. Had this extraordinary man been fortunate enough to have received, in his youth, juster notions of virtue and of vice, he would have

been one of the greatest writers that ever
lived. With this marvellous power of kindling
and giving life to the dormant thoughts of
others, by the seemingly simple, but exquisitely skilful expression of his own, he must,
had he always felt and thought rightly, have
been a most powerful agent for good.

So much has been said upon the more important point, of what Rousseau was, instead
of what he might have been, that I see no
great use in adding to it; but I heartily wish
that some one could be found bold enough to
give to the world a volume extracted from his
confessions, his *promenades solitaires*, his
" Emile,"· and his letters, from which no eye
need turn in alarm, which the purest and
most fastidious taste might be permitted to
admire, and with which the most innocent
heart might sympathize.

But such an attempt would, indeed, require
boldness; for, on the one hand, it would be
met with indignant reprehension by many,
who would see in it nothing but a criminal
effort to familiarize the innocent with the
name and the genius of one whom, not to

know, is to ensure the hearing that "your state is the more gracious—it is a vice to know him;" while, on the other, a host would not be wanting, ready to ridicule the enterprise, and inclined to exclaim, like the Italian language master who was shewn an Ariosto castigato by the mother of one of his pupils,—

"Oh, miladi! Dey have left out de mosti besti parts!"

Nevertheless, I cannot but think that the extraordinary writer who, in these latter days, has been thought the most nearly to approach, by the magic skill of style, to the hitherto inimitable Jean-Jacques—I cannot but think that Madame George Sand would have done better had she prefixed the admirable essay she has just published, as a preface to "the Confessions," to such a compendium as I have mentioned. She, it seems, has thought otherwise; but surely she must, in sitting down to her editorial task, have breathed some such prayer as is put into the mouth of Lady Macbeth, and *effectually* have petitioned the gods to unsex her, in order to prepare for it.

To read this masterly preface without admiration is impossible; but it is equally so to see such a work put forth under the auspices of a woman, without deep regret. This regret is certainly not lessened by the admirable manner in which the character of Jean-Jacques is sketched, in this short but rich little essay. She makes the same admirable distinction, which, if I mistake not, Channing has, in some degree, made before, between *les grands hommes, et les hommes forts;* by which latter class she does not mean to distinguish the hero of the field, but *les hommes d'action*, who have distinguished themselves from their fellow-men by the successful activity of their faculties in any of the busy paths of life. As an illustration of her meaning, she says:

" Jean-Jacques, d'une part, Jean-Jacques le penseur, l'homme de génie et de méditation, *le grand homme*, misérable, injust, et désespéré; de l'autre, Voltaire, Diderot, et les *Holbachiens*, les hommes du jour—désorganisant le société, sans songer sérieusement au lendemain; pensant, dénigrant et philosophant avec le multitude; hommes puissants, *hommes forts*. On les appelait philosophes parce que c'était la mode : tout ce que n'était pas catholique ou protestant s'appelait philosophe. Les *forts* déblayent le chemin, brisent les rochers, percent les forêts ; ce sont les sapeurs de l'ambulante phalange humaine. Les autres (*les grands*) tracent les plans, projettent des lignes au loins, et lancent des ponts sur l'abîme de l'inconnu ; ce sont les ingénieurs et les guides. Aux uns la force de l'esprit, et du caractère, aux autres la grandeur et l'élévation du génie."*

That between Rousseau, and the bold, dashing encyclopædists, there was, on all points of speculation, an immensely wide difference, as

* " Jean-Jacques on one side, Jean-Jacques, the thinker, the man of genius and of meditation, *the great man*, miserable, unjust, and despairing ; on the other, Voltaire, Diderot, and the *Holbachiens*, men of the day—disorganizing society without giving a serious thought to the morrow ; thinking, faultfinding, philosophizing with the multitude ; powerful men, and strong. They were called philosophers, because it was the fashion. Every one who was neither Catholic nor Protestant, called himself a philosopher. The strong men clear the way, excavate the rocks, pierce through forests, and are the sappers and miners of the restless human phalanx. The others (the great men) draw the plans, lay down the distant course, and throw.bridges over the abyss of ignorance. These are the engineers and the guides. To the one belong firmness of character and strength of mind, to the other the grandeur and elevation of genius."

to motive and sincerity of conviction, it is impossible to doubt; and for this, if for nothing else, we must perhaps, in justice, permit Rousseau to remain in the niche assigned to him by George Sand, among the great. He was, as another great writer* truly says, " in earnest;" which is assuredly one most essential material of greatness.

Yet for all this, I cannot join the epithet *great* to the name of Rousseau, without being checked by a feeling that it is inappropriate. Carlyle says of him—

" He is not what I call a strong man," in which all the world, and George Sand among the rest, must agree: but when he adds (and most acutely too) that he is " a morbid, excitable, spasmodic man; at best intense rather than strong," how can we declare him great?

Nevertheless, with a disagreeable vacillation of mind which attends all one's speculations upon Jean-Jacques, one no sooner denies his right to it, than a multitude of splendid passages rise up to the memory, and argue, trumpet-tongued, against the injustice. Perhaps

* Carlyle.

it is this very uncertainty as to the judgment we can conscientiously pass upon him,
which still continues to give us so lively an
interest in all that concerns him.   The spirit,
like an honest judge, wishes for more evidence,
before the final sentence is pronounced, and
cannot therefore pass by with indifference any
object that relates to him.   This may be one
reason why so many pilgrims still yearly climb
the steep path which leads to LES CHARMETTES,
and still linger along the mountain paths
which tradition points out as having been the
most constantly frequented by him.   This may
be one reason.   Another may be found in the
pleasure which is always felt in verifying the
accuracy of a portrait, whether of a landscape
or a face.   And who ever sketched like Rousseau?   But few, probably, have ever felt as
he did the deeply mysterious charm which a
happy combination of natural objects is capable
of producing on the spirits.

There is scarcely any point on which human
beings differ more essentially from each other,
than in their susceptibility to the influence of
this charm.   It appears to be as innate in

some individuals, and as completely absent in others, as is the power of appreciating harmony, or the want of it; and though education may, in both cases, outwardly supply the deficiency, I doubt if all the teaching in the world can make a man feel and enjoy the beauty of the landscape, if *the sense* be not born with him, any more than a defective ear can be taught to detect a false note.

That Jean-Jacques was gifted with this innate appreciation of the beautiful, is a fact that, I presume, no one will venture to dispute, although his descriptions of scenery never in any single instance assume that tone of high descriptive eloquence for which many writers, both in prose and verse, are celebrated. No language in the world, not even that of a child or a peasant, can be more perfect in its simplicity than that which is constantly employed by Rousseau, when describing the scenes he loves; and yet there will result from it so lively a picture, that it leaves a sensation of knowing the place described, more deeply impressed on the reader's mind, that is produced by the written pictures of any other author with whose writings I am acquainted. It is the recollection of these slightly traced, but animated sketches, which yearly sends so many travellers to visit the humble little dwelling called Les Charmettes.

Of the multitudes of English who visit Italy, I should conceive that about three-fourths were people of fortune, or people of fashion, or people laying claim to both, who take the long journey, either because it is *bon-ton* to take it, or because they are tired of England, or because their sons and daughters have particular reasons for wishing to meet the sons and daughters of some other *bon-ton-ists* who have gone thither before them. Of all these, no single individual, I imagine, will be found, who has condescended to make the historic and picturesque little capital of Savoy their *gite* for a night or two, for the purpose of wandering where Jean-Jacques wandered, and for the sake of indulging a little melancholy meditation, within the walls where he sometimes fancied himself so happy, and sometimes knew himself to be so deplorably the reverse:

"What recks it them? What need they? They are sped."

They know that my Lord This and my Lady
That are at Rome, and to Rome they must of
course go too, as fast as bad posters and goodly
mountains will let them.   Les Charmettes!
What on earth can they have to do at Les
Charmettes?   Sleep two nights at Chambéry!
Why should they sleep two nights at Chambéry?—On, courier, on!—Depend upon it
they are right—they could not by possibility
gain anything by the delay, and they might,
par l'impossible, lose their temper.

But, of the other fraction of British wanderers, the objects are very different, and it is
doing them a real kindness to draw their
attention, whenever an opportunity occurs, to
every object that may awaken the imagination,
or touch the heart.   All such will find their
account in paying a visit to Les Charmettes,
despite all the faults and weaknesses of the
man of genius who once made it his home.

I by no means, however, intend to recom-
mend an *étude suivie* of the works of Jean-
Jacques, to all who compose this fourth part
of English travellers; on the contrary, I will
frankly and honestly tell them all that I think

they had much better let it alone. But without this *étude suivie*, they may all venture to know enough of what this " melancholy Jacques" has done to make his name endure as it has done, to render the sight of the dwelling he inhabited, and the scenery he described, profoundly interesting. And truly, unless the pilgrims to Les Charmettes *do* know something about the poor philosopher who followed, with such affecting earnestness, his almost avoided studies beneath the roof of that *triste*-looking little mansion, it will be scarcely worth their while to visit it; for assuredly its being, though close to Chambéry, " retirée et solitaire comme si l'on était à cent lieues," is almost its only charm. Rousseau himself thus describes the place:

" Entre deux côteaux assez élevés est un petit vallon, nord et sud, au fond duquel coule une rigole entre des cailloux et des arbres. Le long de ce vallon, à mi-côte, sont quelques maisons éparses, fort agréable pour quiconque aime un asîle un peu sauvage et retiré. Après avoir essayé deux ou trois de ces maisons, nous choisimes enfin le plus jolie. La maison était très-logeable. Au devant un jardin en terrasse, une vigne au-dessus, un verger au-dessous, vis-à-vis un petit bois de châtaigniers, une fontaine à portée."*

Nothing can be more accurate than this description; and there it is now, to all outward appearance very much the same as it must have been in 1736, when Rousseau, and the woman whom the neglect of his father had made his only protector, and his only resource against absolute starvation, took possession of it.

But although the house itself, and its very ordinary-looking appendages in the way of garden and vineyard, have little beauty or charm of any kind, the view from it is beautiful, and precisely of the character which was likely to enchant such an imagination as that of Jean-Jacques. Mountain rises above moun-

---

* " Between two tolerably high hills is a little valley, north and south, at the bottom of which runs a brook, among pebbles and trees. Along this valley, half way up the hill, are a few scattered houses, very agreeable for such as love a somewhat wild and remote asylum. After having tried two or three of these houses we chose at last the prettiest. The house was very habitable ; before it a terrace-garden, a vineyard above, an orchard below, opposite, a little wood of chesnuts, a fountain close at hand."

tain in the distance, but that distance not very remote, and the ever varying effect of light and shade, produced by the bold and capricious hills thrown about in all directions, and to which every hour of the day gives a new aspect as it passes by, must have made it to him a source of endless enjoyment. Nor was it without deep interest that we trod the path through the vineyard, above the house, which tradition declares to have been his constant morning walk, and the point from whence he saw the sun rise, as he has described it. As this description is very short, I am tempted to transcribe it, for the use of such as may not, *must* not, turn over his forbidden pages in search of a passage which is as bright as the scene it describes; but I will not translate it; I have not the courage, or rather the audacity, to attempt it:

" On le voit," it is the sun of which he speaks, " s'annoncer de loin par les traits de feu qu'il lance au devant de lui. L'incendie augmente; l'orient paraît tout en flammes; à leur éclat, on attend l'astre longtemps avant qu' il se montre: à chaque instant, on croit le voir paraître; on le voit enfin. Un point brillant part comme un éclair, et remplit aussitôt tout l'espace; le voile des ténèbres s'efface et tombe : l'homme reconnait son séjour et le trouve embelli. La verdure a pris durant la nuit une vigueur nouvelle; le jour naissant qui l'éclair, les premiers rayons qui la dorent, la montrent couverte d'un brillant réseau de rosée, qui réfléchit à l'œil la lumière et les couleurs. Les oiseaux en chœur se rèunissent, et saluent de concert le père de la vie; en ce moment, pas un seul ne se tait. Leur gazouillement, faible encore, est plus lent et plus doux que dans le reste de la journée; il se sent de la langueur d'un paisible réveil. Le concours de tous ces objets porte aux sens une impression de fraîcheur, qui semble pénétrer jusqu'à l'âme. Il y a là un quart d'heure d'enchantment, auquel nul homme ne résiste : un spectacle si grand, si beau, si delicieux, n'en laisse aucun de sang-froid."

There is nothing "spasmodic" here, and even Mr. Carlyle himself must, I think, confess that there is something of *greatness* in the writer who can produce a picture so glow-

ing with light and life, in so few and simple words. For myself I confess that, as far
as style goes, I have no power of conceiving
anything more nearly approaching perfection;
and it is such passages as these which account
for and excuse the pertinacious attachment
which has existed through a hundred long years,
and which still continues to exist, for his name,
despite the many clouds which rest upon it.
It was with this picture, and a few others
sketched in the same style, in our thoughts,
that I and my companion set off, after an early
dinner at our comfortable Hôtel de l'Europe,
walk to Les Charmettes.

Chambéry is not greatly celebrated for its
architectural beauty, nor is there much to admire in it, save the picturesque antiquity of
its historical old castle, and the wild beauty of
its Alpine environs. Nevertheless, it is difficult
to ramble about the town in any direction without interest, and the walk aux Charmettes is
full of it from various sources. I never visit
any spot redolent of the memory of those whose
renown has left a train of light behind them
without being struck by the manner in which

every trifle concerning them is hoarded, by even the least enlightened peasant of the neighbourhood.

In naming Rousseau to some labourers at work by the road-side, within a few hundred yards of his residence, they seemed to know him as intimately as if he were living among them still, and one of them, advancing a few steps with us, pointed to a bank of periwinkle, exclaiming, in rather a sentimental tone, " Voilà, madame! Voilà la véritable pervenche!"   And, as the plant is growing precisely on the spot which Rousseau describes as that where Madame de Warens pointed it out to him on their going first to Les Charmettes, it is likely enough to be the *rejeton* of the identical *pervenche* to which he alludes with such a lingering feeling of attachment, when many, many years afterwards he chanced to come upon the same flower, and remembered that she had (vainly) called his attention to it, when they were mounting together the hill which led to the house.

The sort of eloquence with which, by about half a dozen words, he contrives to make one feel the regret with which he looks back to the time when he *might* have looked at it, at her bidding, has certainly been felt and treasured by the generations which have come after him, with more of love and sympathy than was probably ever produced by any other passage equally short and trivial:— convincing proof that when a chord of true feeling is touched, the vibration will extend to everything that is in tune with it.

Had Rousseau conceived an affection as deeply sincere, and as tenaciously constant, to any object within the possible reach of esteem, his exquisitely tender allusions to it would be inexpressibly touching; for never did words more surely echo the very throbbings of the heart, than did those of Rousseau when he speaks of her. Most truly do I believe that all the most essential faults in the character of Rousseau were the effects of this blind, and every way ill-placed attachment. He says himself, of their first interview—

" Cette époque de ma vie a décidé de mon caractère. J'étais au milieu de ma seizième année."

Poor boy! It was a dangerous age to fall into the hands of vice, appearing in the garb of virtue, and never again, as is most painfully evident from every page of his autobiography, never again did he recover any clear notion respecting the difference between right and wrong. He was destitute, and she fed him, and most literally did he worship the benevolence which led her to do so. Of their first meeting, he says—

" C'était les jours des rameaux, de l'année 1728. Je dois me souvenir du lieu; je l'ai souvent depuis mouillé de mes larmes, et couvert de mes baisers. Que ne puis-je entourer d'un balustre d'or cette heureuse place! Que ne puis-je attirer les hommages de toute laterre!"

The man who, at the age of sixty, could thus write, of a woman of whom he has narrated such hateful anecdotes, can scarcely be considered in possession of a perfectly sane understanding; and let us hope that some of the many moral delinquencies to which he has pleaded guilty may be judged leniently, for that reason.

* * * * * *

There are fewer memorials of Rousseau at Les Charmettes, than at Montmorency; at least, there are fewer personal relics. At the Hermitage, you are shown the table at which he wrote the " Heloise," and the old spinette whereby he was wont to soothe himself, by playing the sweet melodies of his own " Devin du village." These, and various other remembrances of him, preserved with the deepest reverence at Montmorency, make one feel more in his presence in the little parlour there, than in the totally unfurnished and desolate-looking rooms at Les Charmettes.

There is still, however, a bower in the little garden, the shrubs of which are doubtless the descendants of those which rendered it *frais et touffu*, when he was wont to take his coffee there " deux ou trois fois la semaine," and near to which was his " autre petite famille, au bout du jardin"—his bees. To the right of the door, a white stone, bearing an inscription, said to be the composition of Madame D'Epinay, was inserted in the wall, by one of the commissioners sent by the Convention of

1792, to the department of Mont Blanc. The inscription is still legible, and is as follows:—

> " Réduit par Jean-Jacque habité,
>   Tu me rapellas son génie,
>   Sa solitude, sa fierté,
>   Et ses malheurs et sa folie.
>   A la gloire, à la vérité
>   Il osa consacrer sa vie
>   Il fut toujours persécuté,
>   Ou par lui-même, ou par l'envie."

The last two lines, at least, have some meaning in them.

The little room in which Rousseau slept is over the vestibule, and its one window is immediately over the door of entrance. If this be the chamber in which he pursued the solitary studies of which he has given so interesting a sketch, and which made, in fact, the most important part of his singularly imperfect education, he must sometimes have been at a loss to find room for the volumes he borrowed from his friends at Chambéry.

Of course, I failed not, according to custom, to look about me for some relic that might remind me of the spot; and I spied a very flourishing patch of *immortelles*, growing beside the gate by which he passed to the part of the garden where he had established the observatory, his nightly use of which so terrified the peasants of the neighbourhood. Could I find a better emblem to remind me of the dwelling of Jean-Jacques? I thought not, and accordingly possessed myself of a handful of the enduring blossoms. On the other side of the little gate was another flower, also in full blossom; it was the "fleur des veuves." And here too was an emblem for me; but not wishing to join *la veuve* to *l'immortel*, in my memory, more than I could help, I left the ominous-looking flower untouched, and giving a last look at the melancholy mansion, turned away, and returned to Chambéry by the path that tradition states to have been the favourite and the daily walk of Jean-Jacques.

AIX-LES-BAINS.

AIX-LES-BAINS.

PART I.

"La Suisse et la Savoie sont deux sœurs jumelles qui se tiennent et se ressemblent, filles de la nature qui les a dotée d'attraits égaux—cependant, de tous les coins de l'Europe les curieux viennent continuellement en Suisse par légions— tandis qu'ils ne font que traverser la Savoie si elle se trouve sur leur chemin."—*L'Italie Pittoresque.*

HAVING enjoyed a few days given to old Chambéry—which one of its veracious chroniclers gravely describes as owing its name to the accident of Noah's Ark having rested, when the waters subsided, upon the point which forms the bold summit of its neighbour Nivolet, whence Cham descended to the plain, and founded the city which still bears his name—having greatly enjoyed a few days in this venerable little capital, we started early, on a bright September morning, for Aix-les-

Bains. The drive is beautiful, and so is the hotel to which it took us, and so was the breakfast, and the flowers that entered with it, and so was the broad terrace beneath our windows, decorated with the loveliest flowering shrubs, in stately boxes, reminding one of the royal orangeries of Versailles; pomegranate, oleander, azalia, cape ˙jessamine, and flowering myrtle, all in perfection, and displaying their delicate beauty under the shelter of the giant mountains that at no great distance formed their back-ground, in most lovely and effective contrast.

Everybody who goes to Aix-les-Bains ought, as I think, to betake himself forthwith to l'Hôtel de la Poste, provided—that is to say, that he can secure rooms looking upon the garden at Guillaud's *third* hotel. From these windows, the combination formed by the craggy termination of the Mont du Chat, and of the richly-cultivated upland beneath, produces one of the most striking pictures imaginable. As usual, we were early in setting out, and as the pretty drive was but a short one, we were early, too, at our beautiful breakfast-table. Numberless wreaths of semi-transparent clouds still hung upon the mountain's side, seeming, from point to point, to be suspended in festoons by the jutting crags that pierced the bristling mass in all directions. The sun tinted those drapery clouds here and there with something of a rainbow colouring, but so fleetingly, that almost before we could exclaim to each other, " How beautiful!" the brightness was past. Vines festooned from tree to tree in every conceivable variety of graceful curve, divided the foreground with groves of acacias and tufted chestnuts; and I remarked one fine catalpa among them, with a lingering bunch or two of blossoms remaining among its broad foliage. It was, in truth, one of those heaven-blessed holiday spots which it is impossible to look upon without a feeling of pious gratitude for having been permitted to do so; and the consciousness of its remoteness from one's ordinary home, adds not a little to this grateful feeling of triumphant joy, at not having lived and died without getting there.

The fulness of my contentment upon this occasion would, I think, have been quite perfect, had it not been for the recollection of sundry dear ones who would have enjoyed it all as keenly as myself and my companion, but whom, I can scarcely hope, will ever make their way thither.   And yet to those who journey from England to Italy by the Mont Cenis, nothing can be much more easy of access.   But I am often astonished at the, to me, preternatural feeling of difficulty which many, with whom I converse, seem to experience at the idea of doing, or seeing anything that would take them a few miles away from the *grande route.*   I often fancy that they must have within them something of that quality of matter which, when it is once propelled, gives it so strong a propensity to go forward in a straight line, that nothing less than a *planetful* of attraction can conquer it; or else it must be such a devoted attachment to the " go-ahead" system as would render every deviation from the direct onward course a positive evil.

*   *   *   *   *   *

Our lingering breakfast ended, and all arrangements made for our accommodation as long as the " Eaux d'Aix" continued to be our head-quarters, we set out as usual to explore; and, to say the honest truth, there is not very much in the town or immediate vicinity of Aix to justify a very ardent recommendation of it, to those who seek to fix themselves at a " watering place" in the intention of being enchanted hourly by the scenery which every lazy half-hour's stroll shall bring before their eyes. Baden-Baden, Ems, or the Baths of Lucca, may do better for such; but to all who will submit to the trouble of either riding or walking for a mile or two in pursuit of their scenery, Aix-les-Bains offers as great attraction as any place I have ever visited. Of the medicinal qualities of its baths, I know nothing, and very little of its social gaieties, for the " season" was well nigh over when we got there. There was still, however, a party of about twenty at the *table-d'hôte*, many of whom were evidently invalids, and one fine-grown, tall young Englishman, had lost the use of his legs; which may lead us to suppose that an ancient rhyme, which I have seen quoted, as applicable to the " Douche" of Aix, may truly describe its qualities.

"Puis par cette eau son corp décrépite,
    Transmué fut par manière subite,
    En jeune gars, frais, gracieux, et droit."

The company talked of balls and belles that had passed away, and of pic-nics that still seemed to be going on among the loiterers that were left. The room in which we dined was a good one, and the dinner excellent, and I was told that the *salle de bal* was elegant and commodious. So much for the accommodations of Aix as a watering-place. The efforts made at all places of summer *rendezvous* to render them attractive, are so very nearly the same everywhere, that it is not necessary to enter more minutely into particulars; but what is not the same everywhere—namely, the never-ending variety of lovely landscape, by which indulgent nature loves to enchant all those of her children who have eyes to see, and hearts to feel her munificence,—of this, as displayed in the neighbourhood of these baths, it may not be lost time to speak, as every hint, faithfully given, which may increase the traveller's power of judiciously choosing his *pied à terre* for summer enjoyment, is worth giving and worth receiving.

The first thing I would remark in favour of Aix-les-Bains is, that notwithstanding the grand and savage wildness, and solemn solitude of many of the scenes in its neighbourhood, it is as well furnished with all the comforts of life as Brighton or Cheltenham; and the next, perhaps more important still, is that, despite its remoteness, it is within the most perfectly convenient reach of all the numerous host of travellers who intend to pass the winter in Italy, but who wish not to approach it too nearly till the first favours of its bright summer are on the wane.

One day, then, having been given to Aix, its hot springs, its cool gardens, &c.; the next was devoted to the Lake of Bourget, and the celebrated Monastery and Mausoleum of Hautecombe. Were this Lake of Bourget at about one-quarter of its actual distance from Aix, the attractions of this remote bathing-place would certainly be very greatly increased, for then one of the loveliest lake-scenes that nature ever produced, would be within reach of its visitors, without putting them to any disagreeable exertion of strength. But as it is, I am fain to confess that the walk, or the donkey-ride from the town to the lake, is much too long to permit such frequent returns to the enchanting shores of Bourget, as all sojourners at Aix would desire. The road, however, is perfectly level, and some part of it sheltered from the sun by an avenue of trees; but these consolations are not sufficient to compensate for the dust, the loss of time, and the fatigue which this long and uninteresting mile and a half of high-road inflicts upon those who would wish never to lose sight of Bourget while remaining in its neighbourhood. But, though on foot, we reached the lake at last, and having gazed upon it very deliberately for some minutes, both my companion and myself ventured to pronounce that it might well bear to be put in competition with any, and every lake we had seen elsewhere, and which truly are not a few.   The seven or eight thousand feet of the Walzmann mountain, which rises with a perpendicular frontage of solid rock from the dark-green waters of the Konigsee, unquestionable give a grandeur to the Austrian lake, which the Savoy one has not; but this feature, though a most noble one, is not wished for, or wanted, at the Lake of Bourget.

Though still on the unsunny side of the Alps, the brightness of the climate we were approaching made itself both to be felt and seen; and though no thrilling majestic mass of rock threw its deep shade over the waters, we were in no humour to lament the loss of it, but condescended to be perfectly well pleased by the Claude-like reflection of the Claude-like sky instead.   In short, while standing on the shore of Lake Bourget, waiting for the boat that was to take us across it to the Abbey of Hautecombe, though we studiously recalled to memory every other lake we had ever seen, we both agreed that we had not the very slightest wish to have any other objects before our eyes than those which we were then gazing on.   Yet at that moment we had by no means seen what was most beautiful in the Lake of Bourget, for it is not till you are well launched upon its bosom, and able to look round upon the magnificent frame of mountains which encloses it, that you become aware of the singularly happy combination of objects which make up the picture. Nothing, to be sure, can be much more unsightly and clumsy-looking than the great, wide, flat-bottomed boat which offers itself to your acceptance on reaching Port-Puer, as they call the bit of ground, looking like a timber-yard, from which you embark; but when you have condescended to enter this rough-looking machine, and have had the rude, but very effective awning stretched over your head, and have discovered the comfort of having a stout rail behind you to lean against, you must be very earnestly bent upon quarrelling with the goods the gods provide, if you do not find yourself superlatively happy and contented.

The difficulty of abstaining from an attempt to describe such scenery as that which blesses

the eye as you cross this lake, after a few
delicious hours have been passed in gazing on
it, is really very great. The mind inevitably
becomes so full of all the images which have
been offered to it, and which it has received
with so much eager avidity as to have left no
room for anything else, that it finds a positive
relief in pouring forth its fulness. But though
I am ready to confess that there may be some
mixture of selfish gratification in describing
what one loves to think of, the attempt to do
it is certainly never made without a good-
natured wish to make all who will listen, share
in the pleasure you have enjoyed. Nay, notwithstanding all the profound criticisms that
have been given to the world, upon the ab-
surdity of attempting to describe what is indescribable, I am of opinion that the reading
of scenes which you have never seen, nor are
ever likely to see, is by no means waste of
time. It is good for us all to know how
bounteous the God of nature has been in
decorating the habitation in which he has
ordained that man shall dwell during his

threescore and ten years of mortal life; it is
good that we should be told of it, if accident
prevents our full acquaintance with the fact
by means of our own experience; and, moreover, by way of encouragement to describers,
it should be remembered that, if among the
dozen who may yawn over their efforts, there
should be one kindled thereby into an energetic determination to look forth upon the
scene himself, the dozen yawners may be very
conscientiously put *in non cale*, for the good
done incontestably exceeds the evil.

Now, then, having made this apology for
myself, let me indulge a little in recalling the
Lake of Bourget, as I saw it, through the
bright clear air of a September morning, while
every imaginable circumstance that could increase the enjoyment which earth, air, and
water have power to give, was in full action.
Nor should the blessing of warmth be left out
of the catalogue, though it would not sound
picturesque, perhaps, to add *fire* to the list of
elements which contributed to the enjoyment
of the scene. But the autumn of Savoy, such

as we saw it during last September, is as
glowing in its warm air and rich colouring as
that of Italy herself. So well did we know
this indeed, that we took care, as usual, to
have a cool hour or two of the morning before
us when we started; for our purpose was to
have a long day of wandering enjoyment; and
we know of old, that the cold chicken and ham
part of the preparation for this, is ..ot more
essentially necessary to its success than the
enlisting in our service the earliest hours of
light. And well on this occasion, as on all
others, were we paid for the trifling exertion
which it requires to leave your bed a little
before you are quite tired of it; for when we
embarked, our course took us westward, and
the effect produced by the rising sun behind
us, upon the majestic range of mountains we
were approaching, was singularly beautiful.
One after another, in just precedence, according to their respective altitudes, point after
point of the Mont du Chat became illuminated
by that indescribable, rose-coloured light,
which seems to belong to Italy, and of which

she lends a gleam now and then to her particular friends and near neighbours. By degrees the smooth bosom of the lake itself began
to reflect the same "celestial rosy red," not,
however, without strong masses of shade still
resting upon it here and there, sometimes from
the tall summit of a mighty mountain, and
sometimes from a tower or a tree, that threw
its firmly-cut *silhouette* upon the water.

The object of our voyage was to reach the
Abbey of Hautecombe, which seems as you
approach it to nestle itself shyly under the
protection of the towering Mont du Chat, that
rises immediately above it. It is, perhaps,
when this delicious little voyage is about half
over, that the beauty of the excursion is at its
height; for by that time, the noble abbey itself
has become a conspicuous feature in the landscape, and the surrounding mountains of Azi,
Grenier, the Mont du Chat, and Nivolet,
together with the hill and castle of Chatillon
at the northern extremity of the lake, may all
be contemplated, as the rowers rest awhile
upon their oars, and discourse to you in a

first-rate style of legendary gossip of all the wonders, not a few of them being considerably *super* the ordinary course of nature, belonging by right immemorial to the principal objects of the landscape.

The elder of our three boatmen—for the heavy craft could not be made to move, I believe, with less—was the greatest orator; but the man evidently second in dignity, never failed to begin talking as soon as his senior ceased, and I was greatly amused by observing the difference which the "march of mind" during the last thirty years (for by so much did their ages differ) had made between them. Though this mental marching has not gone on in the same double-quick time along the "flinty roads of Savoy," as in the highways and byways of England, it was very evident that the education of the younger man had had much more of the modern *positif* in it, than that of the elder. The old man, for instance, made no scruple of telling us, with all the gravity of history, that a certain castle, of which we faintly caught the outline in the dim distance, had been the scene of one of the most remarkable adventures ever known.   It had been destroyed by fire, he said, a good many years ago; he could not state precisely the year; but everybody knew the fact; and that the baron to whom the castle at that time belonged, had two very beautiful daughters, whom he pretended to love very much, but whom he really used very cruelly, never letting them hunt or dance like other young baronesses, but keeping them shut up like prisoners in his castle, and scarcely permitting any of the young knights, who at that time were always riding about the country, to get sight of them.   But he was justly punished for all this; for when the fire happened, the two beautiful young ladies were seen to walk forth in the midst of the flames and the smoke, spring upon two black horses behind two black knights, and gallop away before the eyes of their terrified father and all his household. As they were never heard of afterwards, and as both horses and knights breathed forth fire and flame as violently as the burning castle itself, everybody believed that the devil himself had sent a few of his own combustibles into the castle, and a pair of his own horses, with riders to match, to carry away the young ladies. But be this as it may, there is at least one fact that is perfectly certain—namely, that the blackened walls of the castle and its ramparts are to this day haunted by the departed spirits of the cruel baron and his imprudent daughters, and that none of the country people, far or near, ever venture within sight of the doomed spot after sunset.

END OF VOL. I.

T. C. Savill, Printer, 4, Chandos Street, Covent Garden.

www.ingramcontent.com/pod-product-compliance
Lightning Source LLC
Chambersburg PA
CBHW080550090426
42735CB00016B/3197